The Official Cookbook

The Official Cookbook

Recipes Inspired by Family, Friends, and the T&S Boulangerie Patisserie

Recipes by Lisa Kingsley
Written by S. T. Bende

SAN RAFAEL • LOS ANGELES • LONDON

CONTENTS

Introduction 7

T&S BOULANGERIE PATISSERIE FAVORITES

CHAPTER 1
Pains (Breads)

Tom and Sabine Boulangerie Baguettes 12

Pain d'Epi (Wheat Stalk Bread) 14

Dupain Family-Style Loaves

    Roland's Ancient-Method Loaf 17

    Tom's Modern-Method Loaf 19

Multigrain Bâtard Rolls 20

Brioche à Têtes 23

CHAPTER 2
Pâtisseries (Pastries)

Cat Noir's Chouquettes 27

Tom's Tarte aux Fruits 28

Ladybug Éclairs 31

Galette de Rois (King's Cake) 35

Tom and Sabine Patisserie Croissants 36

CHAPTER 3
Gateaux et Biscuits (Cakes and Cookies)

Candy Apple Cake Pops 40

Pound It! Cake 41

Eiffel Tower Cake 43

Derby Hat Cake 45

Marinette's Birthday Cake 49

Birthday Cake for Adrien 50

Bûche de Noël 53

Tikki's Favorite Chocolate Chip Cookies with Fleur de Sel 57

Lucky Charm and Cataclysm Cupcakes 58

Miraculous Macarons 61

FRIEND AND FAMILY FAVORITES

CHAPTER 4
Apéritifs, Collations, et Boissons (Appetizers, Snacks, and Beverages)

Ladybug Canapés 69

Radishes with Herbed Butter and Salt 70

Cheese Bombs 71

Jagged Stone's Seafood Appetizers

    Shrimp Scampi Skewers 73

    Tiny Tuna Tarts 74

Chocolate Milk Mix 76

Le Grand Paris Sippers 79

CHAPTER 5
Fromage (Cheese) for Plagg

Plagg's Never-Bored Cheese Board 83

Camembert Croque Monsieur 84

Macaroni au Fromage (Macaroni and Cheese) 86

Soupe à l'Oignon Gratinée (French Onion Soup) 87

Fromage Grillé et Soupe à la Tomate
(Grilled Cheese and Tomato Soup) 89

Tartiflette 90

CHAPTER 6
Soupes et Salades (Soups and Salads)

Special-Powers Seaweed Soup 94

Marinette Soup 97

Vichyssoise (Potato-Leek Soup) 98

Salade Parisienne 99

French Bistro Salad 100

CHAPTER 7
Entrées

Sabine's Chicken Cordon Bleu with
Herb-Butter Peas 105

Kung Food's Pepperoni Pizza Sword 107

Cheese-and-Vegetable Pesto Pizza 110

Uncle Wang's Steamed Dumplings 112

Uncle Wang's Shanghai-Style Noodles 115

Sabine's Salmon and Spinach Quiche 116

Colombo de Poulet 119

Hot Dog Dan's Magical Hot Hogs 120

Vincent's Spaghetti 121

Cat Noir's Mashed Potatoes and Sausage 123

Tom's Superhero Brunch

Sweetheart Vol-au-Vents with Wild
Mushroom–Chicken Filling 125

Simple Cheese Soufflé 129

CHAPTER 8
Glaces (Ice Creams)

André Glacier's Ice Creams 132

Dietary Considerations 138

Conversion Tables 139

About The Authors 140

Index 141

INTRODUCTION

Hi, I'm Ladybug—I watch over my hometown of Paris, France, alongside my friend and fellow hero, Cat Noir. Between the two of us, we manage to stay on top of things pretty well—especially when protecting akumatized Parisians from the dastardly supervillain Hawk Moth. Even when things go wrong, I love everything about my city—the people, the fashion, the architecture, the culture, and *especially* the vibrant cuisine! I love spending time with my family and friends while sharing tasty food—particularly the delicious breads, pastries, cakes, and macarons from the finest bakery in all of Paris—Tom and Sabine's Boulangerie Patisserie! It's simply the best.

Along with their daughter Marinette (who's not at all awkward or clumsy, if you ask me), Tom and Sabine Dupain-Cheng work together to create some of the most *divine* sweets in our beloved City of Light at their charming bakery. They also make a variety of *delicious* meals in their own home—many of which are inspired by their friends and family! Whether cooking for their family of three or with their extended family and friends, the Dupain-Chengs can always be counted on to serve up something yummy.

And because the Dupain-Chengs are also simply the *best*, they have created this special cookbook, filled with a collection of their favorite, go-to, family-friendly recipes inspired by their Parisian roots, their loved ones, and their boulangerie patisserie, so you can make their yummy creations in your very own home. The *very* best part: You don't have to be a professional baker to recreate any of these dishes!

Some recipes are sweet, like Pound It! Cake! (page 41). Some are cheesy—Plagg just loves the Camembert Croque Monsieur (page 84)! And some are just plain a-dough-able, as Cat Noir would say. There are plenty of nods to their family traditions—from Roland's Ancient-Method Loaf (page 17) to Uncle Wang's Steamed Dumplings (page 112). And of course, they've added in recipes they tell me were inspired by their own favorite heroes—like Cat Noir's Chouquettes (page 27) and Ladybug Éclairs (page 31)! I have to say that I am honored by the fact that they have named so many of the recipes in this book after me and my friends. As a thank you, Cat Noir and I asked if we could include a few of our favorite dishes, too . . . and they said oui!

I know you're going to love the recipes from the T&S Boulangerie Patisserie Favorites (page 9) and Friend and Family Favorites (page 65) sections every bit as much as I do. If you see me around Paris, be sure to tell me which are your favorites. And if you can't choose just *one*, that's okay—neither can I! Now go out there, get suited up, and start cooking.

Spots on! (And oven mitts too!)

Ladybug

T&S BOULANGERIE PATISSERIE FAVORITES

As the owners of T&S Boulangerie Patisserie, we pride ourselves on serving Paris's best breads, pastries, cakes, and cookies. After all, baking is Tom's passion. His love for all things flour, sugar, and chocolat quite literally drives him from bed in the predawn Parisian hours and powers him throughout the course of the day. He works tirelessly to bring a smile to the faces of our customers—whether through our beguiling baguettes and bâtards, his father's Ancient-Method Loaf (page 17) and his own modern one (page 19), or a macaron-inspired Eiffel Tower cake (page 43) that's an architectural marvel, just like the Tower itself! —*Sabine*

If there's one thing our bakery has shown us, it's that food can truly bring people together . . . and we consider it our great honor to play a part in uniting our friends, families, and you—the honorary citizens of our lovely City of Light! The treats within this section are inspired by our family's Boulangerie Patisserie. There are even some surprises courtesy of our hometown heroes, Ladybug and Cat Noir. —*Tom*

With so many options to choose from, we're sure your table will be brimming with breads—and éclairs and brioches, too!—that will make you the toast of any gathering.

Bon appétit! —*Marinette*

1
PAINS
(BREADS)

There's nothing more quintessentially French than a well-made loaf of bread. From baguettes to brioche, the epicurious flock from all over the world to sample this sumptuous French staple. We've tested many recipes over the years, and we only serve our favorites at the T&S Boulangerie Patisserie—where rolls and loaves fly off the shelves faster than Ladybug and Cat Noir can race across the city. (Though we'll happily save our favorite heroes a baguette any day!) Enjoy baking our tried-and-true treats in your own home. And be sure to save us a slice! —*Tom*

TOM AND SABINE BOULANGERIE BAGUETTES

YIELD: 3 BAGUETTES • V, V+

Baguettes are the heart of any proper French boulangerie. They make the perfect base for a collection of classic dishes—from sandwiches to soups to superhero-themed specialties. But they also make for a delectable treat in and of themselves—particularly when topped with salted butter and jam. The process of making our family's Boulangerie Baguettes begins with a bubbly starter that gets turned into a soft, pliable dough that's then shaped into the classic, slender form. With their crispy crust and airy interior, these baguettes have become our bakery's go-to bread. They're bound to be a hit in your home as well! —*Tom*

STARTER

½ cup cool water

¹⁄₁₆ teaspoon instant yeast or active dry yeast

1 cup artisan bread flour or all-purpose flour

DOUGH

1 cup + 2 tablespoons lukewarm water (85° to 100°F)

1½ teaspoons instant yeast or active dry yeast

1 cup bread flour

2½ cups all-purpose flour, plus more for dusting

2 teaspoons fine sea salt

1. **To make the starter:** In a large bowl, stir together the water, yeast, and flour until well combined. Cover and let stand at room temperature for 12 to 16 hours. The starter should be bubbly and have a pleasant yeasty smell.

2. **To make the dough:** Add the water, yeast, bread flour, all-purpose flour, and salt to the bowl with the starter. Use a wooden spoon to stir vigorously until a soft, mostly smooth dough forms, about 4 to 5 minutes.

3. Transfer the dough to a large, lightly greased bowl. Cover and let the dough rise for 45 minutes. Gently deflate the dough and stretch and fold the edges around the entire ball of dough into the center. Turn the dough over, cover, and let rise for 45 minutes longer.

4. Turn the dough out onto a generously floured work surface. Divide the dough into 3 equal portions. Using lightly floured hands, gently form each dough portion into an 8-by-4-inch rectangle. Dust the surface of the dough lightly with flour. Cover with a clean tea towel and let rest for 30 minutes.

   Tip: *Handle the dough gently to avoid disturbing the air pockets.*

5. Using floured hands, gently pull and roll each dough portion into a 12-inch baguette. Place into greased baguette pans. (If you don't have baguette pans, line a baker's peel or a large rimless baking sheet with parchment. Place the baguettes side by side on the parchment.) Cover and let rise until doubled in size, about 30 to 45 minutes.

6. Preheat the oven to 450°F for 30 minutes. Place a cast-iron skillet on the lowest rack. If you have a baking stone, place it on the middle rack. If you don't have a baking stone, bake the loaf on the parchment-lined baking sheet. Bring 2 cups of water to a boil.

7. Use a bread lame, very sharp knife, or clean razor blade to cut three or four ¼-inch-deep slashes in each baguette. Very carefully transfer the baguettes—parchment and all—to the baking stone. If you don't have a baking stone, bake the loaves on the parchment-lined baking sheet.

8. Pour the boiling water into the cast-iron skillet, close the oven door, and bake until the baguettes are golden brown and sound hollow when tapped on the bottom, about 22 to 28 minutes.

9. Cool on a wire rack.

PAIN D'EPI (WHEAT STALK BREAD)

YIELD: 2 LOAVES • V, V+

Our family's boulangerie is renowned for our breads, including this beautiful bread shaped like a stalk of wheat. While the dough to make pain d'epi is much the same as the dough for a regular baguette, the shape is very different! The "ears" of the wheat stalk are meant to be pulled off (like a roll!) instead of being sliced, making this pretty bread perfect for passing at dinner parties and picnics! Voilà! —*Sabine*

STARTER

¾ cup artisan bread flour

¼ cup lukewarm water (85° to 100°F)

¼ teaspoon instant yeast or active dry yeast

DOUGH

2¼ cups artisan bread flour

¾ cup lukewarm water (85° to 100°F)

¼ teaspoon instant yeast or active dry yeast

1¼ teaspoons fine sea salt

1. **To make the starter:** In a large bowl, stir together the flour, water, and yeast until well combined. Cover with a clean tea towel and let stand at room temperature for 8 to 10 hours. The starter should be bubbly and have a pleasant yeasty smell.

2. **To make the dough:** Add the flour, water, yeast, and salt to the bowl with the starter. Use a wooden spoon to stir vigorously until a soft, slightly shaggy dough forms, about 4 to 5 minutes. Cover and let stand at room temperature for 30 minutes.

3. Gently deflate the dough and stretch and fold the edges around the entire ball of dough into the center. Turn the dough over, cover, and let stand for 30 minutes longer. Repeat the stretching, turning, and 30-minute resting periods two more times.

4. Turn the dough out onto a lightly floured work surface. Divide the dough into 2 equal portions. Using lightly floured hands, gently form each dough portion into a 10-by-4-inch rectangle. Dust the tops of the dough lightly with flour. Cover with a clean tea towel and let rest for 30 minutes.

   Tip: *Handle the dough gently to avoid disturbing the air pockets.*

5. Using lightly floured hands, gently pull and roll each dough portion into a 14-inch baguette. Place the baguettes side by side on a parchment-lined baker's peel or a large rimless baking sheet lined with parchment. Cover with a clean tea towel and let rise until doubled in size, about 45 to 60 minutes.

6. Preheat the oven to 450°F for 30 minutes. Place a cast-iron skillet on the lowest rack. If you have a baking stone, place it on the middle rack. If you don't have a baking stone, bake the loaf on the parchment-lined baking sheet. Bring 2 cups of water to a boil.

continued on next page

14

continued from previous page

7. When the baguettes are doubled in size, use clean, sharp kitchen shears to cut the dough, starting at the bottom of one baguette and working toward the other end. Cut about three-fourths of the way through the dough at a 45-degree angle, then angle the piece of cut dough to one side. Make another cut and angle the piece of dough to the opposite side. Make 8 to 10 cuts per loaf, laying each piece on the opposite side of the one before it.

8. Very carefully transfer the baguettes—parchment and all—to the baking stone. (If you don't have a baking stone, bake the loaves on the parchment-lined baking sheet.) Pour the boiling water into the cast-iron skillet, close the oven door, and bake until the loaves are deeply golden brown and sound hollow when tapped on the bottom, about 25 to 30 minutes.

9. Cool on a wire rack. To serve, the sections of bread can be pulled off like rolls.

DUPAIN FAMILY-STYLE LOAVES

My grandfather is a little old-fashioned in his ways. His favorite saying is "That's not how it's done!" While my father respects his father's methodologies, he's embraced a more modern approach in his baking—one that has led him to alter some of my grandfather's time-honored recipes and has inadvertently caused some conflicts between them. Roland's Ancient-Method Loaf is a nod to my grandfather's traditional way of baking. Our starter uses yeast that's been grown for over two thousand years by our family, beginning with our indomitable ancestor Loafamix the Gaul—but for this recipe, you can use a mix of artisan bread flour, whole wheat flour, and rye flour to make a loaf that is light, airy, and oh-so-delicious. Tom's Modern-Method Loaf is a present-day twist on Roland's Ancient-Method Loaf, offering a nod to the past by using the same artisan bread flour my grandfather uses, but with a slightly different starter and a dusting of rice flour to keep the dough from sticking. —*Marinette*

ROLAND'S ANCIENT-METHOD LOAF

YIELD: 1 LARGE BOULE • V

STARTER

1 cup lukewarm water (85° to 100°F)

½ teaspoon instant yeast or active dry yeast

1¼ cups artisan bread flour

2 tablespoons whole wheat flour

2 tablespoons rye flour

DOUGH

1 cup warm water (105° to 115°F)

¾ teaspoon instant yeast or active dry yeast

1 tablespoon honey

3¾ to 4 cups artisan bread flour

2 teaspoons fine sea salt

1. **To make the starter:** In a large bowl, stir together the water, yeast, bread flour, whole wheat flour, and rye flour until well combined and smooth. Cover with a clean tea towel and let stand at room temperature for at least 2 hours or up to 16 hours. The starter should be bubbly and have a pleasant yeasty smell.

   Tip: *The longer the starter stands, the more flavor your bread will have.*

2. **To make the dough:** Add the water, yeast, honey, 3 cups of the flour, and salt to the bowl with the starter. Stir until well combined and smooth. Let stand for 15 minutes, then stir again. Let stand for 15 minutes longer.

3. Lightly flour a work surface. Turn the dough out onto the surface and knead, adding more flour as necessary to make a soft dough, until the dough is smooth and bounces back when poked with a finger, about 10 to 15 minutes.

   Tip: *My grandfather Roland says to take the dough and fold it in half, rhythmically, pressing it flat, snapping it slightly. It gives it elasticity and develops the gluten in the dough so that it holds together well after it's been baked!*

4. Place the dough in a lightly greased bowl. Cover with a clean tea towel and let rise until nearly doubled in size, about 1½ to 2 hours.

5. Gently deflate the dough and form into a large round ball. Line a baker's peel or large rimless baking sheet with parchment. Lightly flour the parchment and place the dough ball on top. Lightly dust the dough ball with flour. Cover with a clean tea towel and let rise until puffy and about half again as large, about 45 minutes to 1 hour 30 minutes.

6. Preheat the oven to 475°F. Place a cast-iron skillet on the lowest rack. If you have a baking stone, place it on the middle rack. If you don't have a baking stone, bake the loaf on the parchment-lined baking sheet. Bring 2 cups of water to a boil.

continued on next page

continued from previous page

7. Use a bread lame, very sharp knife, or clean razor blade to cut a ¼-inch-deep cross-hatch on the bread. Dust with a little flour. Lower the heat to 425°F. Very carefully transfer the loaf—parchment and all—to the baking stone. Pour the boiling water into the cast-iron skillet, close the oven door, and bake until the loaf is deeply golden brown and sounds hollow when tapped on the bottom, about 25 to 30 minutes. Cool on a wire rack

TOM'S MODERN-METHOD LOAF

YIELD: 1 LARGE BOULE • V, V+

STARTER

1 cup warm water (105° to 115°F)

Pinch of granulated sugar

¼ teaspoon instant yeast or active dry yeast

1 cup artisan bread flour

1 tablespoon rye flour

DOUGH

1 cup warm water (105° to 115°F)

3 to 3¼ cups artisan bread flour

2 teaspoons fine sea salt

½ teaspoon instant yeast or active dry yeast

Rice flour, for dusting

SPECIAL TOOLS

Stand mixer fitted with a dough hook attachment

Fine-mesh strainer

1. **To make the starter:** In a medium bowl, stir together the water, sugar, and yeast. Let stand until the yeast is bloomed and foamy, about 5 to 6 minutes.

2. In another bowl, whisk together the flours. Add to the yeast mixture and stir until well combined. Cover with a clean tea towel and let stand at room temperature for 8 to 16 hours. The starter should be bubbly and have a pleasant yeasty smell.

   Tip: *The longer the starter stands, the more flavor your bread will have.*

3. **To make the dough:** Add the water to the starter and stir to combine. In the bowl of a stand mixer, whisk together 3 cups of the bread flour, salt, and yeast. (If you don't have a stand mixer, use a large bowl.) Pour the starter mixture into the dry flour mixture. Stir to combine. Cover and let the dough rest for about 20 minutes.

4. Attach the dough hook to the mixer. Knead with the dough hook on medium speed for 1½ to 2 minutes until the dough is stretchy and smooth. (If you don't have a stand mixer, turn out onto a floured surface and knead by hand for about 5 minutes.)

5. Place the dough in a lightly greased bowl. Cover with a clean tea towel and let rise until nearly doubled in size, about 2 to 2½ hours.

6. Gently deflate the dough. Cover and let rest for 30 minutes.

7. Form the dough into a large round ball. Line a baker's peel or large rimless baking sheet with parchment. Lightly flour the parchment and place the dough ball on top. Lightly cover and let rise until puffy and nearly doubled in size, about 30 to 45 minutes.

8. Preheat the oven to 450°F. Place a cast-iron skillet on the lowest rack. If you have a baking stone, place it on the middle rack. If you don't have a baking stone, bake the loaf on the parchment-lined baking sheet. Bring 2 cups of water to a boil.

9. Place a little rice flour in a small, fine-mesh strainer and lightly dust the top of the dough ball. Use a bread lame, very sharp knife, or clean razor blade to cut a ¼-inch-deep straight line down the center of the dough ball. Starting at the bottom of the cut, make 2 curved wispy cuts toward the edge of the dough ball on either side of the first cut to create a fern-leaf pattern.

10. Transfer the loaf—parchment and all—to the baking stone. Pour boiling water into the skillet, close the oven door, and bake until the loaf is golden brown and sounds hollow when tapped on the bottom, about 20 to 25 minutes. Cool on a wire rack.

MULTIGRAIN BÂTARD ROLLS

YIELD: 8 LARGE ROLLS OR 12 SMALL ROLLS • V

While enjoying our twentieth anniversary dinner, we overheard a friend saying that our family makes the best bread in the whole of Paris. And while we couldn't pick just *one* loaf to call our favorite, we have to admit that these crunchy, hearty, seeded French rolls are definitely near the top of our list. In making a bâtard—whether it's a large loaf or a smaller roll—the dough is shaped into an oval with slightly pinched ends—a bit like a cross between a round boule and a stick-shaped baguette! Our Multigrain Bâtard Rolls simply fly off the shelves—just like a superhero! —*Sabine*

STARTER

½ cup cool water

⅛ teaspoon instant yeast or active dry yeast

1 cup artisan bread flour or all-purpose flour

1 tablespoon rye flour

DOUGH

⅓ cup millet

Boiling water

1 cup + 2 tablespoons lukewarm water (85° to 100°F)

1½ teaspoons instant yeast or active dry yeast

1½ cups bread flour, plus more for dusting

2 cups whole wheat flour

2 teaspoons fine sea salt

⅓ cup flaxseeds

Cornmeal for sprinkling

EGG WHITE WASH

1 egg white

1 tablespoon water

1. **To make the starter:** In a large bowl, stir together the water, yeast, bread flour, and rye flour until well combined. Cover and let stand at room temperature for 12 to 16 hours. The starter should be bubbly and have a pleasant yeasty smell.

2. **To make the dough:** Place the millet in a small bowl. Pour boiling water over to cover; let stand until just warm to the touch, about 30 to 45 minutes; drain.

3. Add the lukewarm water, yeast, bread flour, whole wheat flour, and salt to the bowl with the starter. Add the softened millet and the flaxseeds. Use a wooden spoon to stir vigorously until well combined. Use your hands to knead the dough in the bowl until it is smooth and bouncy, about 4 to 5 minutes.

4. Cover with a clean tea towel and let rise until doubled in size, about 1½ to 2 hours.

5. Turn the dough out onto a generously floured work surface. Using lightly floured hands, divide the dough into 8 or 12 equal portions. Cover with clean tea towels and let rest for 30 minutes.

   Tip: *Handle the dough gently to avoid disturbing the air pockets.*

6. Line a large rimmed baking sheet with parchment paper. Sprinkle with cornmeal. Using floured hands, gently pull and roll each dough portion into an oval with slightly pointed ends on either side. Place on the prepared pan. Cover with clean tea towels and let rise until puffed, about 45 minutes to 1 hour.

7. Preheat the oven to 425°F. Place a cast-iron skillet on the lowest rack. Bring 2 cups of water to a boil.

8. **To make the egg white wash:** In a small bowl, whisk together the egg white and water.

9. Brush the rolls with the egg white wash. Use a bread lame, very sharp knife, or clean razor blade to cut a ¼-inch-deep slash down the length of each roll. Place the pan on the middle rack. Pour the boiling water into the cast-iron skillet, close the oven door, and bake until the rolls are deep golden brown and sound hollow when tapped on the bottom, about 20 to 25 minutes.

10. Cool on a wire rack.

BRIOCHE À TÊTES

YIELD: 12 SMALL BRIOCHE • V

Made from a soft, sweet dough, these tender, buttery little breads pair well with sweet *and* savory dishes. They're delicious split and smeared with jam and served with your morning café au lait or chocolat chaud (hot chocolate!), as a roll with a lunchtime soup or salad, or as an after-school snack with slice of Brie. "Brioche" means bun in French—and "à tête"? That means "with a head." So those little balls of dough on top are the heads of the buns! You'll find piles of our famous Brioche à Têtes neatly stacked in mouthwatering cases at our family bakery. At least until the morning rush clears them out! —*Marinette*

DOUGH

2¾ cups all-purpose flour, divided

2¼ teaspoons instant yeast or active dry yeast

¼ cup whole milk, warmed (100° to 110°F)

4 large eggs

2 tablespoons granulated sugar

¾ teaspoon fine sea salt

1 cup unsalted butter, at room temperature

EGG WASH

1 large egg

1 tablespoon water

SPECIAL TOOLS

Stand mixer fitted with a dough hook

Brioche pans

Instant-read thermometer

1. **To make the dough:** In the bowl of a stand mixer fitted with a dough hook, combine 1½ cups of the flour and the yeast. Add the warm milk and eggs. Beat at medium speed until smooth. Cover with plastic wrap; let rest for 45 minutes. Add the remaining 1¼ cups flour, sugar, and salt. Use a dough hook to beat on medium speed until the dough is shiny and elastic.

2. With the mixer running, add the butter, 2 tablespoons at a time (make sure it is fully incorporated before adding more). Remove the dough hook. Cover the dough with plastic wrap; let rise for 1 hour. Turn the dough out onto a lightly floured surface; gently fold several times. Place the dough in a lightly greased large bowl. Cover with plastic wrap and refrigerate for 4 to 15 hours.

3. On a lightly floured surface, divide the dough into 12 pieces. Remove a marble-size piece of dough from each larger piece; shape into balls. Shape each larger dough piece into a ball; place in greased brioche pans. Let the marble-size balls and small brioche rise until doubled in size, about 45 minutes to 1 hour.

4. **To make the egg wash:** In a small bowl, whisk together the egg and water.

5. Preheat the oven to 375°F. Grease the round end of a wooden spoon handle (or a clean finger); gently create an indentation in the center of each small brioche. Place the marble-size dough in the indentations. Use a pastry brush to brush the brioche tops with the egg wash.

6. Bake until golden brown and the internal temperature reads 190°F with an instant-read thermometer, about 25 to 30 minutes. Cool on a wire rack.

2
PÂTISSERIES
(PASTRIES)

Our family's bakery has a reputation for having great food, excellent customer service, and the occasional heroic visitor. But it is best known for its truly extraordinary pastries—handcrafted by me, our resident pastry chef, Tom! From croissants to galettes, T&S Boulangerie Patisserie never fails to deliver. And with our hero-inspired treats—Ladybug Éclairs and Cat Noir's Chouquettes—our offerings are extraordinarily super! —*Tom*

CAT NOIR'S CHOUQUETTES

YIELD: 12 PASTRIES • V

Chouquettes—little pieces of choux pastry—are a popular French snack, especially with afternoon coffee or tea. In fact, they're so beloved that the superhero Cat Noir has called them his favorite pastry! To craft these charming bite-size beauties, small portions of choux pastry are topped with pearl sugar and baked into a delectable puff. Light, sweet, and always airy, Cat Noir's Chouquettes are sure to rise like bread to the top of your pastry rankings! —*Marinette*

EGG WASH

1 large egg

1 tablespoon water

CHOUX

1 cup milk

½ cup unsalted butter, cut into ½-inch pieces

2 teaspoons granulated sugar

¼ teaspoon fine sea salt

1¼ cups all-purpose flour

4 large eggs

TOPPING

Pearl sugar

SPECIAL TOOLS

Instant-read thermometer

Electric mixer

Piping bag fitted with a ½- or ¾-inch round tip

1. **To make the egg wash:** In a small bowl, whisk together the egg and water. Set aside.

2. **To make the choux:** Adjust the oven rack to the middle. Preheat the oven to 400°F. Line a large baking sheet with parchment paper.

3. In a 3-quart saucepan over medium-high heat, combine the milk, butter, sugar, and salt, stirring frequently until the butter is melted. Bring to a boil; remove from the heat. Add the flour, stirring vigorously with a wooden spoon or stiff spatula until no lumps remain. Return the pan to medium heat and continue stirring frequently until an instant-read thermometer reads 175°F. (This will take less than 1 minute.)

4. Remove from the heat; let the batter cool to 145°F, stirring occasionally. Add the eggs, one at a time, beating with an electric mixer on medium speed until each egg is fully incorporated before adding the next. Beat for 1 minute after adding the last egg. The batter should be smooth and shiny.

5. Transfer the dough to a piping bag fitted with a ½- or ¾-inch round tip. Pipe into 12 mounds about 1 inch in diameter, 2 inches apart on the prepared baking sheet. Lightly brush the egg wash on each mound. Sprinkle with pearl sugar.

6. Bake until the chouquettes are puffed and deep golden brown, about 20 minutes.

    Tip: *Don't open the oven while the pastries bake; the cool air will prevent them from properly puffing.*

7. Transfer the chouquettes to a wire rack to cool slightly before serving. Serve the chouquettes the same day they are baked.

TOM'S TARTE AUX FRUITS

YIELD: 8 SERVINGS • V

When Marinette has friends over, I make sure to bring in plenty of treats from the bakery. This beautiful fruit tart has been called "delicious" by even the most discerning of our teenage guests! To make your own, start with a traditional pâte sucrée crust and top it with an easy-to-make pastry cream. Carefully arrange concentric circles of fresh fruit and lightly glaze the tops with melted apricot jelly. Comme c'est doux! —*Tom*

PASTRY

1¼ cups all-purpose flour

¼ cup granulated sugar

¼ teaspoon fine sea salt

½ cup cold unsalted butter, cubed

1 large egg yolk

1 tablespoon milk

1 teaspoon vanilla extract

SHORTCUT PASTRY CREAM

One 8-ounce package cold full-fat cream cheese

¾ cup heavy cream

½ cup powdered sugar

1 teaspoon vanilla bean paste or vanilla extract

TOPPING

Fresh fruit, such as halved strawberries, raspberries, peeled and thinly sliced kiwi, mandarin orange segments, and blackberries

¼ cup apricot jelly

SPECIAL TOOLS

Pastry blender

10-inch round tart pan with a removable bottom

1. **To make the pastry:** In a medium bowl, whisk together the flour, granulated sugar, and salt. Cut in the butter with a pastry blender until the mixture resembles coarse crumbs. In a small bowl, whisk together the egg yolk, milk, and vanilla. Stir the egg mixture into the flour mixture; the dough will be crumbly. Transfer the dough to a work surface; gently knead several times.

2. Lightly grease the bottom and sides of a 10-inch round tart pan with a removable bottom. Press the dough into the bottom and up the sides of the pan. Prick the crust with a fork; refrigerate for at least 30 minutes.

3. Preheat the oven to 375°F. Line the crust with parchment paper or foil; fill with dry rice. Bake the crust until set, 12 to 15 minutes. Remove the parchment and rice. Bake until golden brown, 8 to 10 minutes. Cool completely on a wire rack.

4. **To make the shortcut pastry cream:** In a large bowl, combine the cream cheese, cream, powdered sugar, and vanilla. Beat with an electric mixer on medium-high speed until stiff peaks form (tips stand up straight), about 2 minutes. Refrigerate, covered, until well chilled. (The pastry cream can be made up to 3 days ahead.)

5. Spread the pastry cream over the cooled bottom crust.

6. **To make the topping:** Place fruit in concentric circles on the pastry cream, beginning with the strawberries, then kiwi, mandarin oranges, and raspberries. Fill the center with blueberries.

7. In a small bowl, heat the apricot jelly. Use a pastry brush to gently brush the jelly on the fruit. Chill the tart for 1 hour before serving.

LADYBUG ÉCLAIRS

YIELD: 10 TO 12 ÉCLAIRS • V

Our hometown heroine is always on hand to protect our beloved city. And we couldn't think of a more fittingly French tribute than to create an éclair in her honor! Ladybug Éclairs take the classic Parisian pastry and throw in a decidedly *super* twist. Pâte à choux is injected with pastry cream, then coated with an elegant chocolate ganache. Topped off with an edible sugar ladybug, a Ladybug Éclair is a tasty tribute that's been crafted with our most heartfelt gratitude. Merci, Ladybug! —*Tom*

SHORTCUT PASTRY CREAM

Two 8-ounce package cold full-fat cream cheese

1½ cups heavy cream

1 cup powdered sugar

2 teaspoons vanilla bean paste or vanilla extract

EGG WASH

1 large egg

1 tablespoon water

CHOUX

1 cup water

½ cup unsalted butter, cut into ½-inch pieces

2 teaspoons granulated sugar

½ teaspoon fine sea salt

1 cup all-purpose flour

4 large eggs

GANACHE

One 8-ounce bar semisweet chocolate, chopped

1 cup heavy cream

TOPPING

10 to 12 edible sugar ladybug decorative toppers

SPECIAL TOOLS

Electric mixer

Instant-read thermometer

Piping bag fitted with a large round pastry tip

Piping bag filled with a smaller round tip

1. **To make the shortcut pastry cream:** In a large bowl, combine the cream cheese, cream, powdered sugar, and vanilla. Beat with an electric mixer on medium-high speed until stiff peaks form (tips stand up straight), about 2 minutes. Refrigerate, covered, until well chilled. (The pastry cream can be made up to 3 days ahead.)

2. **To make the egg wash:** In a small bowl, whisk together the egg and water. Set aside.

3. **To make the choux:** Adjust the oven rack to the middle. Preheat the oven to 425°F. Line a large baking sheet with parchment paper.

4. In a 2-quart saucepan over medium-high heat, combine the water, butter, granulated sugar, and salt, stirring frequently until the butter is melted. Bring to a rolling boil; remove from the heat. Add the flour, stirring vigorously with a wooden spoon or stiff spatula until no lumps remain. Place the pan over medium heat and cook, stirring frequently, until an instant-read thermometer reads 175°F., or until a spoon can stand in the center of the dough. (This will take about 2 to 3 minutes.)

5. Remove from the heat; let the dough cool to 145°F, stirring occasionally. Add the eggs, one at a time, beating with an electric mixer on medium speed until each egg is fully incorporated before adding the next. Beat for 1 minute after adding the last egg. The dough should be smooth and shiny.

6. Transfer the dough to a piping bag fitted with a large round pastry tip. Lightly brush the parchment on the prepared pan with water. Pipe ten to twelve 5-inch-long logs ½ to ¾ inch in diameter about 2 inches apart on the prepared baking sheet. Use a water-moistened finger to gently smooth any peaks. Lightly brush the egg wash on each log. Bake for 20 minutes. Lower the oven temperature to 375°F. Bake until golden brown, about 18 to 20 minutes longer. Turn oven off and let pastries sit in oven for 15 minutes. Remove from oven

continued on next page

continued from previous page

and poke each pastry with a skewer or toothpick to allow steam to escape. Transfer to a wire rack to cool completely.

7. **To make the ganache:** Place the chocolate in a medium heatproof bowl. In a small saucepan, warm the cream over medium-low heat until it reaches a simmer (do not let it boil). Pour the cream over the chocolate; let stand for 2 minutes. Stir the mixture until the chocolate is melted and the ganache is smooth.

8. Transfer the chilled pastry cream to a piping bag fitted with a small round tip. Use a toothpick to make a hole in one end of each éclair shell. Gently insert the piping tip into the hole. Pipe the pastry cream into the shell; stop when it feels full.

9. Dip the top of each éclair in the ganache; place on a wire rack. Place a ladybug on top of each éclair. Let sit until the ganache is set (1 hour at room temperature or 30 minutes in the refrigerator), or until ready to serve. Refrigerate filled éclairs in an airtight container for up to 3 days; unfilled shells can be refrigerated for up to 5 days.

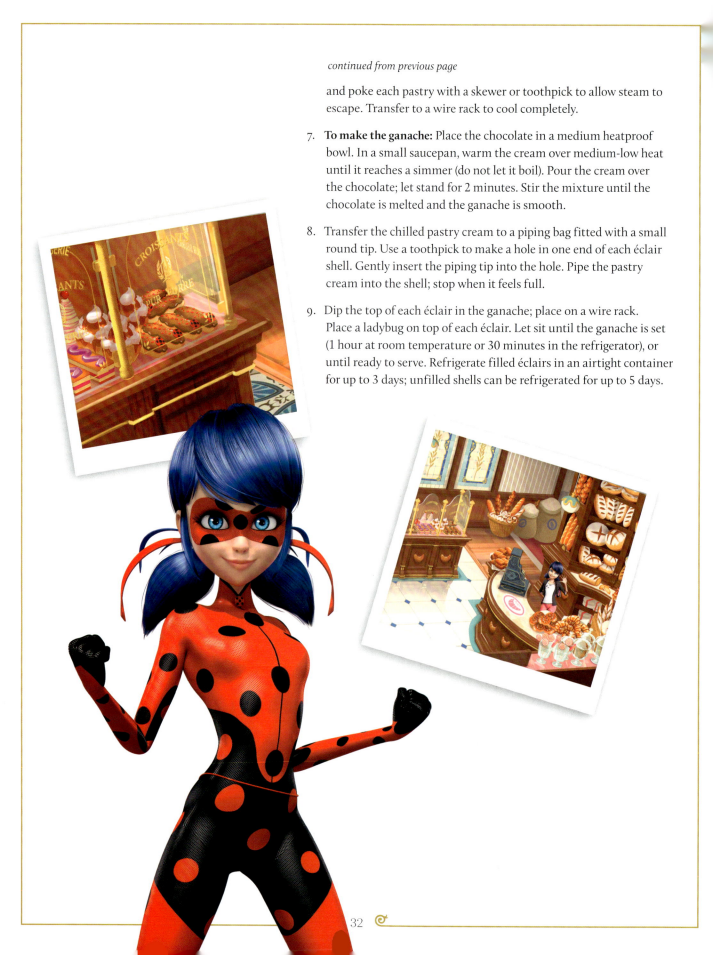

GALETTE DE ROIS (KING'S CAKE)

YIELD: 16 SERVINGS • V

Grandpa Roland and Dad might not always agree on which type of flour to use—or the method by which their breads are best baked. But one thing this traditional baker and his more modern son *can* agree on is that a galette should melt in the mouth yet *also* remain perfectly crispy. For King's Day, the pair teamed up to make a galette that is the perfect alliance of tradition and modernity. To make this delightful dessert in your own home, carefully mold puff pastry around a homemade almond frangipane filling. Score the pastry in a circular pattern, brush with a syrupy glaze, and you'll have a galette that's fit for a king. —*Marinette*

FRANGIPANE

6 tablespoons unsalted butter, cubed, at room temperature

½ cup powdered sugar

1 cup almond flour

1 teaspoon orange zest

¼ teaspoon fine sea salt

2 large eggs, at room temperature

¼ teaspoon vanilla extract

¼ teaspoon almond extract

1 whole almond, for the fève

PASTRY

One 17.2-ounce box frozen puff pastry (2 sheets), thawed, well chilled

GLAZE

1 egg yolk

1 teaspoon milk

SPECIAL TOOL

Electric mixer

1. **To make the frangipane:** In a large bowl with an electric mixer, beat the butter and powdered sugar on medium speed until light and smooth. Beat in the almond flour, zest, and salt until combined. Beat in the eggs, vanilla, and almond extract until well combined. Cover and chill for 1 hour.

2. **To prepare the pastry:** Line a large baking sheet with parchment paper. On a lightly floured work surface, roll one sheet of puff pastry into a 9½-inch circle. Place on the prepared baking sheet; cover with plastic wrap. Repeat with the remaining sheet of puff pastry; place on top of the plastic wrap. Cover the top pastry with plastic wrap. Chill for 30 minutes.

3. Preheat the oven to 375°F.

4. Remove the frangipane and pastry from the refrigerator. Remove the top pastry; set aside. Spread the frangipane over the bottom pastry, leaving a 1-inch border. Place the almond (anywhere) in the frangipane. Brush the border with water. Place the second pastry circle on top; press down the edge to seal well. Flute the edge.

5. **To make the glaze:** In a small bowl, whisk together the egg yolk and milk. Lightly brush the top of the galette with the glaze; do not let the glaze drip on the edge. Use a sharp paring knife to make a crisscross pattern on top. Cut a few small slits on top to allow steam to escape during baking.

6. Bake until deep golden brown, about 30 minutes. Slide the galette onto a wire rack to cool. (The galette deflates as it cools.) Serve warm or at room temperature.

TOM AND SABINE PATISSERIE CROISSANTS

YIELD: 12 CROISSANTS • V

Croissants are quintessential French food. With their light, airy dough and crispy, flaky exterior, it's no wonder they fly off the shelves of our family bakery! Our classic patisserie croissants are complicated to make, so for our cookbook, we've decided to offer a simplified, accessible twist on the popular Parisian pastry. To make pain au chocolat, sprinkle some chopped semisweet chocolate onto the pastry wedges before rolling them up (Step 4), and you'll have a variety of delightful treats right at your fingertips. —*Sabine*

1¼ teaspoons instant yeast or active dry yeast

½ cup warm water (105° to 115°F)

2½ cups all-purpose flour, divided

6 tablespoons heavy cream

2 tablespoons + 2 teaspoons granulated sugar

1 egg

2 tablespoons unsalted butter, melted

¾ teaspoon fine sea salt

½ cup cold unsalted butter

EGG WASH

1 egg

1 tablespoon water

SPECIAL TOOL

Pastry blender

1. In a medium bowl, dissolve the yeast in the warm water. Let stand until foamy, about 5 minutes. Add ½ cup of the flour, cream, sugar, egg, melted butter, and salt. Use a wooden spoon to beat vigorously until smooth; set aside.

2. In a large bowl, using a pastry blender, cut the cold butter into the remaining 2 cups flour until pieces are the size of dried kidney beans. Add the yeast mixture. Stir gently until the mixture is completely moistened, without breaking up the pieces of cold butter.

3. Cover and chill in the refrigerator for at least 12 hours or up to 3 days.

4. When ready to bake, line 2 large rimmed baking sheets with parchment paper. Divide the dough into 2 portions. On a lightly floured surface, roll 1 portion into a 14-inch circle (keep the other portion chilled until needed). Cut the circle into 6 wedges. Starting at the outer edge, roll each wedge loosely toward the point. Place the croissants, point sides down, on the prepared baking sheet. Repeat with remaining dough portion and second baking sheet. Cover lightly and let rise until nearly doubled in size, about 2 to 2½ hours.

5. Preheat the oven to 325°F.

6. **To make the egg wash:** In a small bowl, beat together the egg and water. Brush the egg wash over the croissants.

7. Bake until lightly browned, about 20 to 22 minutes. Serve warm or let cool on wire racks.

3
GATEAUX ET BISCUITS
(CAKES AND COOKIES)

The grand finale of any meal is dessert. And for our patisserie, there are no finer finishes than our patrons' favorite cakes and cookies. From our famed Eiffel Tower Cake (an architectural masterpiece, just like its namesake!) to a broad array of birthday cakes, these recipes make for a sweet send-off after a night spent among friends. —*Marinette*

CANDY APPLE CAKE POPS

YIELD: 24 CAKE POPS • V

Although we love to bake the everyday staples that fuel the families of Paris, we're equally partial to seasonal specialties—from Bastille Day baguettes to Christmas logs, and of course, anything heart-shaped we can serve around Valentine's Day. Our Candy Apple Cake Pops are a St. Valentine favorite and a fun twist on the heart-shaped candied apples we've served in years past. To make this cake-pop version, just press a moldable mixture of apple cake crumbles and frosting into heart-shaped silicone molds. Freeze, then dip the hearts in a cinnamon-flavored candy coating (be sure to tint it red first!). Brush with luster dust to create a sparkling, sweetened, apple-flavored treat that will please family members and patisserie patrons alike. —*Tom*

One 13.25-ounce box spice cake mix

1¼ cups unsweetened applesauce

½ cup canned vanilla frosting

Nonstick cooking spray

One 12-ounce bag red candy
    coating melting wafers

¼ teaspoon cinnamon candy flavoring

Red edible glitter spray

SPECIAL TOOLS

24-cavity (13-by-10-inch) silicone
    heart-shaped mold

24 paper cake pop sticks

1. Preheat the oven according to the cake mix directions. Grease a 9-by-13-by-2-inch cake pan.

2. Prepare the cake mix according to the package directions, substituting the applesauce for the oil and eggs. Pour the batter into the prepared cake pan. Bake until a toothpick inserted into the center of the cake comes out clean, about 25 to 30 minutes. Cool completely in the pan.

3. Crumble the cake into a large mixing bowl. Stir in the vanilla frosting with a fork until well combined and the mixture holds together in small balls. With dampened hands, shape into twenty-four 1½-inch balls. Spray the silicone heart mold with nonstick spray. Press the balls into the molds. Freeze for 1 hour or until firm enough to remove from the mold.

4. Meanwhile, place the candy coating wafers in a medium microwave-safe bowl. Microwave for 1 minute; stir. Continue to microwave in 30-second intervals, stirring after each, until all the candy coating is melted. Stir in the cinnamon flavoring. Pop the cake hearts out of the mold and onto a work surface. To attach a stick to a cake heart, first dip the end of a stick (½ inch) into the melted candy coating. Push the candy end of the stick into the center of a cake heart. Place on a parchment-lined baking sheet. Repeat with the remaining cake hearts and sticks. Chill for 30 minutes.

5. Reheat the candy coating if necessary. Holding the stick, dip a cake heart in the melted candy coating. Allow excess coating to drip off before returning to the parchment paper. Repeat with the remaining cake hearts. Chill the dipped hearts until hardened, about 30 minutes.

6. Before serving, spray the hearts with a little edible glitter for some sparkle and shine.

POUND IT! CAKE

YIELD: 8 SERVINGS • V

Bakers are known for their love of butter, but this fact is especially true in the case of *French* bakers. After all, butter is at the heart of almost every beloved French recipe. And it's guaranteed to make any treat, from croissants to tarts, even more flavorful. Pound It! Cake is a rich, buttery pound cake that's been infused with hints of orange and vanilla. It's a satisfyingly zesty treat that can be casually served with coffee or tea, or dished out as a celebratory dessert after the impressive defeat of a seasoned supervillain. And just like Ladybug and Cat Noir, it comes with its very own salutation: Pound It! —*Tom*

1 cup unsalted butter, at room temperature

1 cup granulated sugar

4 large eggs, at room temperature

2 cups all-purpose flour

1 tablespoon orange zest

½ teaspoon fine sea salt

½ cup whole milk, at room temperature

1 teaspoon vanilla extract

Powdered sugar, for serving

SPECIAL TOOLS

Electric mixer

Fine-mesh sieve

1. Preheat the oven to 350°F. Lightly grease a 9-by-5-inch loaf pan.

2. In a large bowl with an electric mixer on medium speed, beat the butter until light and creamy. Beat in the granulated sugar until well combined. Add the eggs, one at a time, and beat until thoroughly mixed before adding the next. After the last egg is added, beat until the mixture is light and fluffy, about 5 minutes.

3. In a small bowl, stir together the flour, zest, and salt. In a 1-cup glass measuring cup, stir together the milk and vanilla. Alternating, add the flour mixture and the milk mixture to the butter mixture, beginning and ending with the flour mixture.

4. Pour the batter into the prepared pan, spreading it evenly. Bake until a long toothpick inserted into the center comes out mostly clean, about 1 hour. (Tent the cake with foil about halfway through baking if it appears to be browning too quickly.) Transfer to a wire rack to cool for 5 minutes. Turn out of the pan and cool completely on a wire rack.

5. Wrap the loaf in plastic wrap; store for 1 day before serving. To serve, use a fine-mesh sieve to dust the top with powdered sugar.

EIFFEL TOWER CAKE

YIELD: 8 TO 10 SERVINGS • V

Perhaps the most impressive dessert commissioned at the Boulangerie Patisserie is the Eiffel Tower Cake we baked for Mrs. Chamack. Crafted from flour, sugar, eggs, and vanilla, and covered in traditional French macarons, it was a structural masterpiece just like the Tower itself. This flat-lying version is just as tasty . . . though it's considerably easier to sculpt *and* transport. To make the Eiffel Tower Cake at home, carve a homemade vanilla cake into the shape of the Eiffel Tower, cover it with French buttercream, and top it with blue, pink, and yellow "macarons" cut from an easy-to-make homemade marshmallow fondant. This Eiffel Tower Cake becomes an impressive display of French craftsmanship and artistry—just like La Tour Eiffel! —*Sabine*

MARSHMALLOW FONDANT

One 16-ounce package marshmallows

2 tablespoons water

8 cups powdered sugar, divided, plus more for dusting

Vegetable shortening, for greasing

Gel paste food coloring: brown, blue, pink, and yellow

FRENCH SPONGE CAKE

4 large eggs

2 cups cake flour or all-purpose flour

2 teaspoons baking powder

1 cup whole milk

4 tablespoons unsalted butter, cut into pieces

2 cups granulated sugar

1 tablespoon vanilla extract

FRENCH BUTTERCREAM

1 cup granulated sugar

6 tablespoons water

10 egg yolks

2 cups unsalted butter, at room temperature

1 tablespoon vanilla extract

⅛ teaspoon fine salt

Brown gel paste food coloring

1. **To make the marshmallow fondant:** Place the marshmallows and water in a large microwave-safe bowl. Microwave on high for 1 minute; stir. Microwave in 30-second intervals, stirring after each, until the marshmallows are just melted and smooth. Stir in 5 cups of the powdered sugar. Grease the work surface with a little vegetable shortening. Turn the mixture out onto the greased surface. Grease your hands; knead the mixture, working in the remaining 3 cups of powdered sugar to make a smooth, thick consistency. The fondant should hold the shape of a ball but still be workable. Divide the fondant into four portions. Knead brown, blue, pink, or yellow food coloring into each portion to achieve the desired color. Wrap in plastic wrap and let stand for 1 to 2 hours or until cooled completely and firm enough to roll out.

2. **To make the sponge cake:** Let eggs stand at room temperature for 30 minutes. Preheat the oven to 350°F. Grease a 13-by-9-inch cake pan. Line the bottom of the pan with parchment paper. Grease the paper and lightly flour the entire pan; set aside.

3. In a medium bowl, whisk together the flour and baking powder; set aside. In a medium saucepan over low to medium heat, heat the milk and butter just until the butter is melted; set aside.

4. In a large mixing bowl, beat the eggs with an electric mixer on high speed until slightly thickened, about 4 minutes. Very gradually beat in the sugar, beating on medium-high speed until pale yellow and thickened, about 5 minutes. Add the flour mixture; beat on low speed until just combined. Gradually add the warm milk mixture, beating on low speed until just combined. Beat in the vanilla. Scrape down the sides of the bowl as needed.

5. Pour the batter into the prepared baking sheet. Bake until a toothpick inserted into the center comes out clean, 30 to 35 minutes. Cool the cake in the pan on a wire rack.

ingredients and recipe continued on next page

continued from previous page

SPECIAL TOOLS

Electric mixer

Candy thermometer

Stand mixer

4 disposable piping bags

1-inch cookie cutter

6. **To make the French buttercream:** In a medium saucepan over medium-high heat, combine the sugar and water. Cook and stir until a candy thermometer reads 240°F.

7. Meanwhile, in the large bowl of a stand mixer on high speed, beat the egg yolks until slightly thickened and lemon-yellow colored, about 4 minutes. When the sugar mixture has reached 240°F, gradually pour in the hot syrup with the mixer running. Scrape down the sides of the bowl. Continue to beat on high speed until the mixture is very light and fluffy and has cooled to room temperature, about 10 minutes. With the mixer running on medium-low speed, add the softened butter very gradually, 1 tablespoon at a time, beating well after each addition. The mixture may look curdled, but it will become smooth in the end. Beat in the vanilla and salt. If the mixture is still looking curdled, beat longer to warm it until smooth. If the mixture is too soupy, chill for 15 minutes and beat again. Tint the buttercream a medium golden-brown color.

8. When cake is completely cool, remove the cake to a serving platter; discard the parchment paper. Starting 3½ inches from the corner at a 9-inch end of the cake, use a small, sharp knife to cut a curved line down the long side of the cake that ends at the bottom corner of the opposite 9-inch side of the cake. Repeat on the other side to create an Eiffel-Tower–shaped cake. Reserve cake trimmings for another use.

9. Frost top and sides of the cake with buttercream, spreading it as smooth as possible. Chill the cake for 30 minutes to firm up the buttercream before decorating.

10. **To decorate the cake:** Roll out the brown fondant. Cut out two ½-inch-wide strips, one 4-by-5-inch oval, and a 2-by-3-inch trapezium. Cut the oval in half the long way. Place pieces on cake as shown in photo (page 42), trimming the strips to end at the edge of the cake. Roll out the blue, pink, and yellow fondant and cut 1-inch circles to represent macarons using a miniature cookie or biscuit cutter. Arrange on cake as desired.

11. Serve the cake at room temperature. If not serving immediately, store in the refrigerator.

DERBY HAT CAKE

YIELD: 10 TO 12 SERVINGS • V

I am *very* passionate about design. I've spent hours sketching, stitching, and mocking up many creations. A while ago, I worked hard to create a derby hat that would be worthy of winning a design contest—and when my friend Tikki told me that designing a derby hat would be a "piece of cake," I had an idea to merge my passion for design with my passion for baking! Inspired by that off-the-cuff remark, I've whipped up a stylish and tasty recipe for Derby Hat Cake. This two-layer vanilla almond cake is filled with strawberry mousse and decorated with black fondant. Trimmed into the shape of a bowler, and absolutely *brimming* with flavor, this cake is destined to be the absolute height of fashion! —*Marinette*

CAKE

3¼ cups sifted cake flour

1½ tablespoons baking powder

¼ teaspoon fine salt

14 tablespoons unsalted butter, room temperature

1¾ cups granulated sugar

1 cup + 2 tablespoons whole milk

1½ teaspoons vanilla extract

1½ teaspoons almond extract

5 large egg whites, at room temperature

STRAWBERRY MOUSSE FILLING

One 8-ounce package cream cheese, at room temperature

1 cup canned strawberry cake and pie filling

1½ cups frozen whipped topping, thawed

STRAWBERRY FROSTING

1 cup vegetable shortening

2 teaspoons clear vanilla extract

4 cups sifted powdered sugar

2 tablespoons milk, plus more as needed

½ cup canned strawberry cake and pie filling

1. **To make the cake:** Preheat the oven to 350°F. Grease two 8-inch round cake pans; line the bottoms of the pans with parchment paper circles. Grease the parchment paper and lightly flour the pans; set aside.

2. In a large mixing bowl, whisk together the cake flour, baking powder, and salt; set aside.

3. In the large bowl of a stand mixer on medium speed, beat the butter until fluffy, about 1 minute. Gradually add the granulated sugar, beating on medium-high speed until pale and very fluffy, about 4 minutes. Decrease the speed to low. Add the flour mixture one-third at a time, alternating with the milk and beating until just combined after each addition. Add the vanilla and almond extracts and beat until combined.

4. In a large clean mixing bowl with an electric mixer on medium-high speed, beat the egg whites until stiff peaks form. Gently fold about one-quarter of the beaten egg whites into the cake batter to lighten. Fold in the remaining egg whites until well combined and no streaks remain. Divide the batter evenly between the prepared cake pans, spreading to smooth the surface.

5. Bake on the middle rack until a toothpick inserted into the center of the cakes comes out clean, 25 to 30 minutes. Cool in the pans for 10 minutes. Remove the cakes from the pans and cool on a wire rack.

6. **To make the strawberry mousse filling:** In a medium mixing bowl with an electric mixer, beat the cream cheese until creamy, 30 seconds to 1 minute. Beat in the strawberry filling. Beat for 3 minutes or until fluffy. Fold in the whipped topping. Immediately spoon the filling over the top of one of the cake layers; spread to the edges of the cake. Top with the second cake layer. With a long metal spatula, smooth any excess filling to make the edges of the cake and the filling smooth and straight. Cover with plastic wrap and chill for at least 2 hours or until the filling is firm.

7. Use a serrated knife to trim the top edge of the cake to create a dome shape.

ingredients and recipe continued on next page

continued from previous page

MARSHMALLOW FONDANT

One 16-ounce package marshmallows

2 tablespoons water

8 cups powdered sugar, divided, plus more for dusting

Vegetable shortening for greasing

Black food coloring

Silver luster dust

SPECIAL TOOLS

Stand mixer

Electric mixer

2- or 3-inch teardrop-shaped cookie cutter

8. **To make the strawberry frosting:** In a large mixing bowl with an electric mixer on high speed, beat the vegetable shortening and vanilla for 30 seconds. Gradually beat in 2 cups of the sifted powdered sugar. Beat in the milk. Gradually beat in the remaining 2 cups of sifted powdered sugar and enough additional milk to reach piping consistency. Add the strawberry cake filling and beat until smooth. Spread a thin layer of strawberry frosting over the cake sides and top. Transfer to a serving platter; cover with plastic wrap and chill until ready to decorate.

   Tip: To save time, you can beat together canned white frosting with the strawberry cake filling to create a simpler strawberry frosting.

9. **To make the marshmallow fondant:** Place the marshmallows and water in a large microwave-safe bowl. Microwave on high for 1 minute; stir. Microwave in 30-second intervals, stirring after each, until the marshmallows are just melted and smooth. Stir in 5 cups of the powdered sugar. Grease the work surface with a little vegetable shortening. Turn the mixture out onto the greased surface. Grease your hands; knead the mixture, working in the remaining 3 cups of powdered sugar to make a smooth, thick consistency. The fondant should hold the shape of a ball but still be workable. Knead in the food coloring to achieve the desired color. Wrap in plastic wrap and let stand for 1 to 2 hours or until cooled completely and firm enough to roll out.

10. **To decorate the cake:** Lightly dust a work surface with powdered sugar. Roll the black fondant into a 14-inch circle, about ¼ inch thick. To transfer the fondant sheet to the cake, carefully roll it onto a rolling pin, then unroll it over the top of the cake, centering the fondant circle over the cake and allowing the fondant sheet to drape evenly down the sides. (There should be excess fondant around the base of the cake.)

11. With cupped hands, gently press and smooth the fondant onto the sides of the cake, letting the extra fondant at the base turn out onto the serving plate. Trim the extra fondant to about 1½ inches wide all around the cake to create the brim of the hat. Reroll the trimmed fondant on the lightly dusted work surface to ⅛ inch thick. Using a 2- or 3-inch teardrop-shaped cookie cutter, cut out about two dozen teardrop shapes. Lightly brush the back of the shapes with a little water and attach to the top and partially down the sides of the cake, overlapping slightly. If desired, roll out some fondant and cut into a 1-inch-wide ribbon. Wrap around the base of the hat and attach with a little brush of water. Cut two feather shapes from the fondant and "fringe" the edges with a fork. Let dry 8 hours or overnight. Store the decorated cake in the refrigerator while the feathers are drying. When dry, brush feathers with a little silver luster dust. Attach feathers to cake with a brush of water.

MARINETTE'S BIRTHDAY CAKE

YIELD: 14 TO 16 SERVINGS • V

For our little girl's fourteenth birthday, we had to make the loveliest cake ever. After all, Marinette deserves the best—and this recipe is nothing if not that! To craft this confection, we baked a three-tiered pink confetti cake and frosted it in pink icing—one of Marinette's favorite colors. Topped off with raspberries or strawberries and a generous smattering of sprinkles, Marinette's Birthday Cake is one for the ages. Joyeux anniversaire, Marinette! —*Tom*

CONFETTI CAKE

4 egg whites, in 4 separate cups

½ cup unsalted butter

2 cups cake flour or all-purpose flour

1 teaspoon baking powder

½ teaspoon baking soda

½ teaspoon fine salt

1¾ cups granulated sugar

1⅓ cups buttermilk

1 teaspoon clear vanilla extract

Few drops neon pink food coloring

½ cup multicolored sprinkles or nonpareils

STRAWBERRY FROSTING

1 ounce freeze-dried strawberries

1 cup unsalted butter, at room temperature

4 cups sifted powdered sugar

3 tablespoons whole milk, plus more as needed

1 teaspoon vanilla extract

DECORATION

1 cup canned vanilla frosting (optional)

Pink food coloring (optional)

Multicolored sprinkles or nonpareils

Raspberries or small whole strawberries

SPECIAL TOOLS

Electric mixer

Food processor or bullet-style blender

1. **To make the confetti cake:** Let egg whites and butter stand at room temperature for 30 minutes. Grease and lightly flour one 8-inch round cake pan, one 6-inch round cake pan, and one jumbo cupcake tin (3½ inches). In a medium bowl, stir together flour, baking powder, baking soda, and salt; set aside. Preheat oven to 350°F.

2. In a large bowl with an electric mixer on medium-high speed, beat the butter for 30 seconds. Gradually add the granulated sugar, beating until fluffy, about 3 minutes. Add the egg whites, one at a time, beating well after each addition. Alternately add the flour mixture and the buttermilk, beating on low speed after each addition, until just combined, scraping down the sides of the bowl as needed. Beat in the vanilla and food coloring. Fold in the sprinkles. Evenly fill each of the prepared pans three-quarters full.

3. Bake until a toothpick inserted into the center of the cakes comes out clean, about 20 to 30 minutes. Cool in the pans for 10 minutes. Remove the cakes from the pans and cool completely on a wire rack. If necessary, trim the tops of the cakes to make them flat.

4. **To make the strawberry frosting:** In a small food processor or blender, pulse freeze-dried strawberries to a fine powder; set aside.

5. In a large bowl, beat the butter with an electric mixer on medium-high speed for 30 seconds. Add the powdered sugar, strawberry powder, milk, and vanilla. Beat on low speed for 1 minute to combine. Beat on medium-high speed until fluffy, about 2 to 3 minutes. Add more milk, if necessary, to create the desired consistency. Spread the frosting on the tops and sides of all 3 cakes.

6. **To decorate the cake:** If using, place the canned frosting in a microwave-safe bowl. Microwave for 10 seconds; stir. If the frosting is not pourable, microwave for another 10 seconds. Stir in enough pink food coloring to make the frosting darker than the strawberry frosting. Spoon melted frosting along the top edges of the frosted cakes, allowing some to drip down the sides a little. Decorate with sprinkles. Stack the cakes on top of each other on a serving plate. Garnish the edges of each cake with berries.

BIRTHDAY CAKE FOR ADRIEN

YIELD: 14 TO 16 SERVINGS • V

We love to spoil Marinette's friends with our culinary creations, and we took great joy in creating a birthday cake for her charming classmate Adrien. This particular recipe yields a two-tiered passion fruit chiffon cake. Filled with pastry cream and strawberries, and covered in whipped cream and fresh strawberries, Birthday Cake for Adrien is sweet, classic, and oh-so-French—just like Adrien himself. —*Sabine*

CAKE

5 egg yolks

8 egg whites

2 cups all-purpose flour

1¼ cups granulated sugar

1 tablespoon baking powder

1 teaspoon fine sea salt

¾ cup passion fruit juice blend

½ cup light olive oil

1 teaspoon vanilla extract

½ teaspoon cream of tartar

FILLING

One 8-ounce package cream cheese, at room temperature

½ cup powdered sugar

¾ cup heavy cream

1 teaspoon vanilla extract

1 cup chopped strawberries

½ cup passion fruit pulp

WHIPPED-CREAM FROSTING

2 cups heavy cream

¼ cup sour cream

1½ cups powdered sugar

Pink gel paste food coloring

GARNISH

Whole fresh strawberries

SPECIAL TOOLS

Electric mixer

Pastry bag fitted with medium round tip

1. **To make the cake:** Let the egg yolks and whites stand at room temperature for 30 minutes. Grease two 8-inch and two 6-inch round cake pans; set aside. In a large mixing bowl, stir together flour, granulated sugar, baking powder, and salt. Make a well in the center of the flour mixture; set aside.

2. Preheat the oven to 325°F.

3. Add the egg yolks, juice, olive oil, and vanilla to the flour mixture. Beat with an electric mixer on low speed until combined. Beat on medium-high speed until smooth, about 4 to 5 minutes.

4. In a very large bowl and with clean beaters, beat the egg whites and cream of tartar on medium speed until stiff peaks form. Gradually add the batter to the beaten egg whites, folding in by hand with a rubber spatula until no white streaks remain. Divide the batter among the prepared cake pans (even thickness of batter in each pan). Bake until a toothpick inserted into the center of each cake comes out clean, about 20 to 25 minutes. Cool completely in the pans.

5. **To make the filling:** In a medium mixing bowl, beat the cream cheese and powdered sugar until smooth, 30 seconds to 1 minute. Beat in the heavy cream and vanilla. Beat until fluffy, 2 to 3 minutes. Fold in the chopped strawberries and passion fruit pulp.

6. To assemble the cake, remove the cakes from the pans. Spread about two-thirds of the filling on top of one of the 8-inch layers; top with the remaining 8-inch cake layer. Spread the remaining one-third filling over one of the 6-inch cake layers; top with remaining 6-inch cake layer. Cover the cakes with plastic wrap and chill for at least 1 hour.

7. **To make the whipped-cream frosting:** In a large mixing bowl with an electric mixer on low speed, beat the heavy cream, sour cream, and powdered sugar until combined, about 1 minute. Beat on medium speed until soft peaks form, about 5 minutes. Reserve about ¾ cup of the mixture and tint to desired shade of pink with food coloring.

continued on next page

continued from previous page

8. Place the filled 8-inch cake on a serving platter. Frost the top and sides with the white whipped-cream frosting. Place the filled 6-inch cake on top of the larger cake. Frost the top and sides of the 6-inch cake.

9. **To garnish the cake:** Cut about half of the strawberries in half; arrange around base of small cake. Slice remaining half of strawberries and arrange aroiund base of larger cake. Place a few halved nad sliced strawberries on top of cake. Place the tinted frosting in a pastry bag fitted with a medium round tip. Pipe decoratively around the edges of the cakes.

10. Keep refrigerated until ready to serve, up to 4 hours.

BÛCHE DE NOËL

YIELD: 10 TO 12 SERVINGS • V

Christmas is one of our favorite times of year. Come December, the entire city of Paris becomes a wintry wonderland, with decorations adorning every shop and street. Our family likes to celebrate by gifting our customers special log-shaped Christmas cakes, or Yule logs, that we bake just for the holiday. They make for a festive feast—one we'd share with the world, if we could! If you don't live close enough to pick up this special cake from our Boulangerie Patisserie, you can bake your own Bûche de Noël. This version is made by covering a thin sheet of chocolate sponge cake in peppermint whipped cream and rolling it, jelly-roll–style, into a log. It's glazed with chocolate ganache and decorated with sugared cranberries and rosemary and cocoa-dusted meringue mushrooms—to resemble the logs you might find in the forest! It's a perfect dessert for Christmas Eve or any time around the holidays. We simply adore our Bûche de Noël. It's so delicious, it might just be considered a Christmas miracle. Joyeux Noël! —*Marinette*

CAKE

5 eggs, separated

Vegetable shortening for greasing

¾ cup unsweetened cocoa powder, divided

½ cup + ⅓ cup granulated sugar

3 tablespoons vegetable oil

¼ cup strong-brewed coffee

1 teaspoon vanilla extract

⅔ cup all-purpose flour

1 teaspoon baking powder

¼ teaspoon baking soda

¼ teaspoon kosher salt

PEPPERMINT WHIPPED FILLING

4 candy canes or 20 striped peppermint hard candies, coarsely broken, plus more for decorating

8 ounces cream cheese, softened

½ cup heavy cream

Pink gel paste food coloring (optional)

1. **To make the cake:** Let the egg yolks and whites stand at room temperature for 30 minutes. Preheat the oven to 350°F. Grease a rimmed 10-by-15-inch baking sheet with vegetable shortening. Line the pan with parchment paper, overlapping and folding as necessary to cover the bottom and two of the sides. Grease paper and dust with 2 tablespoons of the cocoa powder; set aside.

2. In a large mixing bowl with an electric mixer on medium-high speed, beat the egg yolks and ½ cup of the granulated sugar until slightly thickened and light in color, about 3 minutes. Add the oil, coffee, and vanilla; beat on low speed to combine. In another bowl, whisk together the flour, ½ cup of the cocoa powder, baking powder, baking soda, and salt. Add to the yolk mixture; beat on low speed until combined.

3. Wash the beaters thoroughly and place the egg whites in a large, clean bowl. Beat on high speed until soft peaks form. Gradually add the remaining ⅓ cup sugar, 1 tablespoon at a time, beating constantly. Continue to beat until stiff peaks form. With a rubber spatula, fold the beaten egg whites into the chocolate batter, one-third at a time, until well combined and no streaks of egg white remain. Spread the batter evenly in the prepared pan. Bake until the cake bounces back when touched in the center, about 12 to 15 minutes.

4. Place the remaining 2 tablespoons of cocoa powder in a fine-mesh sifter. Sift the cocoa powder evenly over the entire top of the cake. Invert the pan and cake onto a large, clean kitchen towel. Remove the pan and parchment paper. Roll up the cake (with the towel) starting at one of the short edges. Cool the rolled cake for 30 minutes. Unroll the cake and allow the cake to cool completely. (It is helpful if the cake remains partly curved at one end from rolling and is not flat.)

ingredients and recipe continued on next page

continued from previous page

SUGARED CRANBERRIES AND ROSEMARY

$\frac{1}{4}$ cup fine sanding sugar

1 egg white

$\frac{1}{3}$ cup cranberries

3 to 5 rosemary sprigs

MERINGUE MUSHROOMS

1 egg white

Pinch of cream of tartar

$\frac{1}{4}$ cup granulated sugar

1 tablespoon unsweetened
   cocoa powder

CHOCOLATE GANACHE GLAZE

8 ounces bittersweet
   chocolate, chopped

1 cup heavy cream

2 tablespoons light corn syrup

SPECIAL TOOLS

Electric mixer

Fine-mesh sifter

Blender

Disposable piping bag

5. **To make the peppermint whipped filling:** Place the candy canes in a blender; pulse to a fine powder. Set some of the powder aside to decorate the cake, if desired. Place the cream cheese in a medium mixing bowl. Add the peppermint powder. Beat with an electric mixer on medium speed until the mixture is combined. Beat in heavy cream. Beat for 2 minutes, until light and fluffy. Beat in pink food coloring, if desired. Spread on the cooled cake, leaving a $1\frac{1}{2}$-inch border of unfrosted cake at the curled end. Beginning at that end, roll up the cake snugly (without the towel) to make a round log. Place the cake on a wire rack. Chill while preparing the decorations.

6. **To make the sugared cranberries and rosemary:** Place the fine sanding sugar in a small bowl. In another bowl, beat the egg white with a fork just until foamy. Lightly brush the cranberries and rosemary sprigs with the egg white and dip them into the sanding sugar. Set aside to dry, about 1 hour.

7. **To make the meringue mushrooms:** Preheat the oven to 200°F. Line a baking sheet with parchment paper.

8. In a medium mixing bowl with an electric mixer on medium-high speed, beat the egg white and cream of tartar until soft peaks form. Gradually beat in the granulated sugar. Beat for 2 to 3 minutes or until stiff peaks form. Beat in the cocoa powder. Place the meringue in a disposable piping bag. Snip a $\frac{1}{2}$-inch opening at the tip of the bag. Pipe the meringue onto the prepared baking sheet in the shapes of caps and upright stems. Use wet fingertip to pat down any peaks on the cap pieces. Bake until dry and firm, about 1 hour. Turn off the oven (do not open the door) and let dry in the oven for another hour. To assemble a mushroom, use a little chocolate ganache to attach the stem pieces to the caps.

9. **To make the ganache glaze:** Place the chocolate in a medium bowl. In a small saucepan over medium-high heat, bring the cream and corn syrup to a boil. Pour over the chocolate. Let stand until the chocolate is melted, about 5 minutes. Whisk until smooth. Pour and spread the glaze over the cake log, allowing excess glaze to drip off. Transfer the cake to a serving plate. Sprinkle with the reserved crushed peppermint candy, if desired. Chill the glazed cake for 1 to 4 hours before serving. Just before serving, garnish with the sugared cranberries, sugared rosemary, and meringue mushrooms. Slice with a serrated knife.

TIKKI'S FAVORITE CHOCOLATE CHIP COOKIES WITH FLEUR DE SEL

YIELD: 24 COOKIES • V

My lovely friend Tikki has a pretty pronounced sweet tooth. Her favorite food is a chewy chocolate chip cookie, and after many months of testing, I came up with the *perfect* recipe to please her palate! Eggs, flour, and two kinds of sugar are whipped into a subtly sweet batter, then mixed with chocolate chips and sprinkled with thick flakes of sea salt. These gooey, chocolatey treats are perfect for teatime, after-school snacking, or sharing with your friends and their favorite superheroes! —*Marinette*

1 cup unsalted butter, melted and slightly cooled

¾ cup packed brown sugar

½ cup granulated sugar

1 large egg

1 large egg yolk

1 teaspoon vanilla extract

2½ cups all-purpose flour

1 teaspoon kosher salt

½ teaspoon baking soda

½ teaspoon baking powder

One 12-ounce package semisweet chocolate chips

Fleur de sel

SPECIAL TOOLS

Electric mixer

Cookie scoop

1. Preheat the oven to 350°F. Line 2 large baking sheets with parchment paper.

2. In a large bowl with an electric mixer on medium speed, beat the butter, brown sugar, and granulated sugar until well combined. Beat in the egg, yolk, and vanilla until light and creamy, about 2 minutes.

3. In a medium bowl, stir together the flour, salt, baking soda, and baking powder. Gradually add to the butter mixture, beating just until combined. Fold in the chocolate chips.

4. Use a medium cookie scoop to scoop the dough onto the baking sheets, spacing them 2 inches apart. Bake until the edges are golden brown, 9 to 11 minutes. Lightly sprinkle the cookies with fleur de sel. Let cool on the baking sheets for 5 minutes. Transfer the cookies to a wire rack to cool completely.

LUCKY CHARM AND CATACLYSM CUPCAKES

YIELD: 24 CUPCAKES • V

Paris's resident superheroes have very different powers. While Ladybug can summon a Lucky Charm to help her battle any bad guy, Cat Noir activates the Cataclysm, a destructive power that throws his enemies off their guard. As a nod to two heroes with *very* different abilities, we created the perfect pair of specialty cupcakes. Both Lucky Charm and Cataclysm Cupcakes are made from a base of sweet vanilla batter, though a hearty dose of cocoa powder is added to the latter. They're topped with hero-specific decorations—red frosting for Ladybug's yo-yo, and green to make Cat Noir's cataclysmic cat print. Simultaneously sweet and supremely heroic, Lucky Charm and Cataclysm Cupcakes will have lucky diners exchanging joyful fist bumps—just like our heroes. Pound It! —Sabine

CUPCAKES

2½ cups all-purpose flour

2 teaspoons baking powder

½ teaspoon baking soda

½ teaspoon fine salt

½ cup + 2 tablespoons milk

½ cup vegetable oil

1 teaspoon vanilla extract

½ cup unsalted butter, at room temperature

1 cup granulated sugar

3 large eggs

3 tablespoons cocoa powder

DECORATION

One 16-ounce can vanilla frosting

Red no-taste food coloring

Neon green food coloring

Black Marshmallow Fondant, homemade (page 47) or store-bought

SPECIAL TOOLS

Electric mixer

Piping tip

2-inch paw-shaped cookie cutter

Piping bag

1. **To make the cupcakes:** Preheat the oven to 350°F. Line 24 muffin cups with paper or foil liners.

2. In a medium mixing bowl, whisk together the flour, baking powder, baking soda, and salt. In a small bowl, combine ½ cup of the milk, oil, and vanilla.

3. In a large mixing bowl with an electric mixer on medium speed, beat the butter for 30 seconds. Gradually add the sugar and continue to beat until light and fluffy, about 3 minutes. Beat in the eggs, one at a time, scraping down the sides of the bowl as needed. With the mixer on low, alternately add the flour mixture and the milk mixture, beating just until combined after each addition. Use an ice cream scoop to fill half of the lined muffin cups with vanilla batter, filling almost to the top.

4. Add cocoa powder and the remaining 2 tablespoons of milk to the remaining batter. Stir until well combined. Use an ice cream scoop to fill the remaining lined muffin cups almost to the top. Bake for 15 to 20 minutes, or until a toothpick inserted into the center of a cupcake comes out clean. Remove the cupcakes from the pans and cool on a wire rack.

5. **To decorate:** Divide the frosting evenly between two small microwave-safe bowls. Stir the red food coloring into one bowl of frosting and the green coloring into the other bowl. Place one bowl in the microwave and microwave for 10 seconds, or until slightly melted. Stir the frosting. Repeat with the other bowl of frosting. Dip the tops of the vanilla cupcakes in the red frosting. Return to the cooling rack to set up. Dip the tops of the chocolate cupcakes in the green frosting. Let cool on the rack.

6. On a piece of parchment paper, roll out the black fondant to ⅛ inch thick. Using a large straw or piping tip, cut out 60 small rounds (about ½ inch). Using a 2-inch paw-shaped cookie cutter, cut out 12 paw shapes. To decorate the Ladybug cupcakes, use a table knife or metal spatula to score a line down the center of the red icing to make wings. On each red cupcake arrange 5 fondant rounds on the wings for spots. For the Cat Noir cupcakes, place a fondant paw shape on top of each of the green frosted cupcakes.

MIRACULOUS MACARONS

YIELD: ABOUT 3 DOZEN MACARONS PER VARIATION • V, GF

According to Cat Noir, our patisserie has the best macarons in Paris! That's high praise, considering how notoriously difficult it is to bake this well-loved treat. Not only must a macaron's ingredients be kept at the perfectly proper temperature—and the batter stirred with unparalleled precision—but the cook time and temperature must be *extremely* exact. It's no wonder many a baker has crumbled beneath the pressure of preparing such a delicacy. Luckily, our patisserie is known throughout the city for its miraculous macarons. They come in a variety of flavors—from Pistachio to Lemon to Marinette's Macarons (the pink strawberry variety reminiscent of Marinette's signature color!). And with a few helpful tips, you'll be whipping up this notoriously complex treat with ease. Quel régal! —*Tom, Sabine, & Marinette*

Note: *This recipe is partially written in metric weight measurements for accuracy, which is very important when making macarons. Read through the recipe and tips before beginning.*

COOKIES

100 g egg whites (about 3 large egg whites)

130 g powdered sugar (about 1 cup)

140 g almond flour (about 1½ cups)

¼ teaspoon cream of tartar

90 g granulated sugar (about ½ cup)

Food coloring (optional)

1 teaspoon vanilla or almond extract

FRENCH BUTTERCREAM*

½ cup granulated sugar

3 tablespoons water

5 egg yolks

1 cup unsalted butter, at room temperature

1 teaspoon vanilla or almond extract

Pinch of fine salt

SPECIAL TOOLS

Fine-mesh sifter

Electric mixer

Large piping bag with a medium round tip

Candy thermometer

Stand mixer

Piping bag with a medium round or star tip

1. **To make the cookies:** Let the egg whites stand at room temperature for 30 minutes. Line 2 large rimmed baking sheets with parchment paper.

   Tip: *If your environment is humid, partially dry out the egg whites the day before you are baking. Place the measured egg whites in a bowl; cover the bowl with plastic wrap. Poke a few tiny holes in the plastic wrap. Refrigerate overnight before using.*

2. Sift the powdered sugar and almond flour together into a bowl. Place the egg whites in a very clean, large mixing bowl.

   Tip: *Use a scale to measure the egg whites, almond flour, and sugars. Use an almond flour that has been pre-sifted and is very fine.*

3. Beat the egg whites with an electric mixer on medium-high for 30 seconds, until foamy. Add the cream of tartar. With the mixer on medium-high speed, very gradually beat in the granulated sugar. Beat in the food coloring, if using, and the vanilla extract, almond extract, or other flavoring (see variations). Beat on high speed until the mixture is very stiff. Peaks should stand up straight.

   Tip: *Be sure to beat the egg whites until they are very stiff. When you make peaks in the stiff meringue, the tips should not bend at all. A stand mixer works best.*

4. With a rubber spatula, fold one-third of the almond flour mixture into the egg whites. Fold in the remaining almond flour mixture. Continue to fold the batter until it changes texture and becomes more pourable. It should fall off the spatula and be able to form a figure eight without breaking. Spoon into a large piping bag with a medium round tip.

   Tip: *When piping the batter, hold the bag perpendicular to the baking sheet, pulling straight up to finish. Do not try to tap down any peaks that are left from piping. If the batter is the correct consistency, the rounds will be nearly flat.*

continued on next page

continued from previous page

5. Pipe 1½-inch rounds 1½ inches apart onto the prepared baking sheets. Tap the baking sheets on the counter several times to release any large air bubbles. Let stand until the tops look dry before baking, about 40 minutes.

    Tip: *The resting time can take longer in humid environments and less time in dry ones. The rounds should lose their shiny appearance and look dull or matte.*

6. Preheat the oven to 300°F.

7. Bake the cookies until puffed and dry-looking, about 12 to 15 minutes, rotating the baking sheets halfway through the baking time. Cool completely before removing from the parchment paper.

8. **To make the French buttercream:** In a small saucepan over medium-high heat, combine the granulated sugar and water. Cook and stir until a candy thermometer reads 240°F.

9. Meanwhile, in the large bowl of a stand mixer on high speed, beat the egg yolks until slightly thickened and lemon-yellow colored, about 4 minutes. When the sugar mixture has reached 240°F, gradually pour in the hot syrup with the mixer running. Scrape down the sides of the bowl. Continue to beat on high speed until the mixture is very light and fluffy and has cooled to room temperature, about 10 minutes. With the mixer running on medium-low speed, add the softened butter very gradually, 1 tablespoon at a time, beating well after each addition. The mixture may look curdled, but it will become smooth in the end. Beat in the vanilla and salt. Place the buttercream in a piping bag with a medium round or star tip.

    Tip: *If the mixture is still looking curdled, beat longer to warm it until smooth. If the mixture is too soupy, chill for 15 minutes and beat again.*

10. To fill the macarons, pipe some filling onto the back of one of the macaron shells. Sandwich with another macaron shell, back facing in. Store the filled macarons, covered, in the refrigerator for 1 to 2 days before serving. The filling will soften the shells for a better eating texture.

    Pistachio Variation: Decrease the almond flour to 100 g. Add 30 g of finely ground pistachios to the almond flour mixture when sifting. If desired, add a little green and yellow food coloring to the beaten egg whites.

    Raspberry/Strawberry/Blueberry Variations: Add 2 tablespoons of fine strawberry powder, raspberry powder, or blueberry powder to the almond flour

mixture when sifting. Add a few drops of pink and/or purple food coloring to the batter in Step 4, if desired. Beat ¼ cup of the desired seedless fruit preserves (strawberry, raspberry, blueberry) into the prepared French buttercream.

Marinette's Macarons Variation: Prepare the Strawberry Variation except do not add the food coloring to the egg whites. After folding is complete and the correct texture is achieved, remove about ¼ cup of the batter to a piping bag with a small round tip. Add red food coloring to the remaining batter and pipe as directed onto the baking sheets. Pipe tiny dots of the plain batter on top of the pink rounds. Bake as directed.

Chocolate Variation: Decrease the almond flour to 100 g. Add 30 g of unsweetened cocoa powder to the almond flour mixture when sifting. Fill chocolate macarons with Dark Chocolate Buttercream*.

Lemon Variation: Substitute lemon flavoring for the vanilla and use yellow food coloring. Beat ⅓ cup of purchased lemon curd into the buttercream.

Coconut Variation: Place ½ cup of finely shredded unsweetened coconut in a food processor or blender. Process until finely ground. When preparing the macarons, substitute coconut flavoring for the vanilla. For Ladybug macarons, add red food coloring to the egg whites. For Cat macarons, add neon green food coloring to the egg whites. Add the finely ground coconut when folding in the almond mixture. Bake as directed. Fill coconut macarons with Dark Chocolate Buttercream*. Decorate the tops of the filled macarons with some piped black icing to make dots or paw prints.

Passion Fruit Variation: Prepare passion fruit curd. In a small saucepan over medium heat, combine ⅓ cup strained passion fruit pulp (fresh or frozen), ½ cup granulated sugar, 4 egg yolks, 5 tablespoons unsalted butter, and a pinch of salt. Cook and stir until thickened and bubbly. Transfer to a bowl; cover the surface with plastic wrap and chill for 1 hour or until completely cool. Beat into the prepared buttercream. When making macarons, add a little purple food coloring. Fill the macarons with the passion fruit buttercream.

*__Note:__ *For Dark Chocolate Buttercream, prepare the buttercream as directed above. In a double boiler, melt 4 ounces of bittersweet chocolate. Cool until just warm. Beat into the prepared buttercream on low speed until well combined.*

FRIEND AND FAMILY FAVORITES

The recipes in this section honor the many different groups that make up our family—from our biological family to our friend family to the found family we've created over the years. —*Marinette*

We've included our go-to favorites—from Sabine's Chicken Cordon Bleu with Herb-Butter Peas (page 105) to Simple Cheese Soufflé (page 129). And we've thrown in recipes inspired by beloved members of our extended and chosen family—like the Cheese-and-Vegetable Pesto Pizza (page 110), which pays homage to my father, Roland, and Le Grand Paris Sippers (page 79), inspired by our dear friend (and accomplished chef!) Marlena. We've even included recipes submitted by our favorite superheroes—like Cat Noir's Mashed Potatoes and Sausage (page 123). —*Tom*

With dishes covering everything from appetizers to ice cream and spanning the ages from generational recipes to Caribbean-style cuisine, this section serves up a variety of comfort foods that will appeal to friends and family the world over. —*Sabine*

4
APÉRITIFS, COLLATIONS, ET BOISSONS
(APPETIZERS, SNACKS, AND BEVERAGES)

Whether cooking a meal for family, friends, or superheroes, our family knows that a good appetizer can set the mood for an altogether excellent evening. The dishes in these pages— from Ladybug Canapés to Cheese Bombs—and accompanying beverages have earned rave reviews from Marinette, her friends, and our favorite heroes. We know you'll enjoy them every bit as much as we do! —*Sabine*

LADYBUG CANAPÉS

YIELD: 18 CANAPÉS • V

When problems arise in our hometown, a familiar, red-and-black hero swoops in to save the day. We're talking, of course, about Paris's very own Ladybug! She's done so much for our town, we wanted to honor her with this delicious recipe—complete with a crafty nod to Ladybug's penchant for polka dots and all things fabulous. Ladybug Canapés top a quintessential French baguette with garlic-herb cream cheese and cherry-tomato-and-black-olive ladybugs. Rich, creamy, and sure to bring people together, these appetizers pack a fashionably powerful punch—just like their namesake hero. —*Tom*

4 ounces cream cheese, at room temperature

⅓ cup sour cream

Black gel paste food coloring

2 teaspoons minced fresh chives

1 teaspoon minced fresh dill

1 tablespoon minced fresh parsley

⅛ teaspoon garlic salt

18 slices Tom and Sabine Boulangerie Baguette (page 12), lightly toasted

9 cherry tomatoes, quartered

9 large pitted black olives, halved widthwise

Thirty-six 1½-inch-long pieces fresh chive

1. In a small bowl, stir together the cream cheese and sour cream until smooth. Transfer 2 tablespoons to another small bowl and tint black. Place the tinted cream cheese mixture in a small plastic bag; set aside.

2. Add the chives, dill, parsley, and garlic salt to the remaining cream cheese mixture. Spread on the baguette slices. Place 2 tomato quarters on each to form the ladybug wings. Place 1 olive half on each baguette to form the head. Place 2 chives into the olives to make the antennae.

3. Snip a very small hole in the corner of the plastic bag and pipe spots onto the wings (you will have extra).

RADISHES WITH HERBED BUTTER AND SALT

YIELD: 8 SERVINGS • V

Our family is in agreement—Ladybug's signature suit is a spotted masterpiece. Its delicate design and high-contrast patterns mark the absolute height of style, which, in a fashion-forward place like Paris, makes it more than deserving of its own special dish. With its surplus of toppings set along a fabulously French base, Radishes with Herbed Butter and Salt offer a visual nod to our favorite hero—and to the very simple French appetizer of radishes with plain butter and salt. Simply prepare Tom and Sabine Boulangerie Baguettes (page 12) and top lightly toasted slices with herb butter and thinly sliced radishes for a contemporary take on the classic French hors d'oeuvre. —*Sabine*

½ cup unsalted butter, at room temperature

1 scallion, finely chopped

1 tablespoon finely chopped fresh basil

1 teaspoon finely chopped fresh thyme leaves

1 teaspoon lemon zest

Freshly ground black pepper

16 slices Tom and Sabine Boulangerie Baguette (page 12), lightly toasted

1 bunch assorted radishes, thinly sliced

Flaky salt

1. In a medium bowl, stir together the butter, scallion, basil, thyme, lemon zest, and black pepper to taste. Spread on the toasted baguette slices. Arrange on a serving platter.

2. Just before serving, arrange the radish slices on the baguette slices. Sprinkle with flaky salt.

CHEESE BOMBS

YIELD: ABOUT 72 PUFFS • V

These gougères, or as our family likes to call them, Cheese Bombs, are an incredibly popular snack among our family and friends, who clamor for these cheese-infused savory pastries. To craft this delicacy, we infuse our dough with Gruyère, mustard, and nutmeg. This makes for a fabulous medley of flavorful fromage—one that's bound to knock anyone off their feet. No explosives necessary! —*Marinette*

1 cup water

½ cup whole milk

½ cup unsalted butter, cubed

¼ teaspoon fine sea salt

1½ cups all-purpose flour

5 eggs

6 ounces Gruyère cheese, shredded

1 tablespoon Dijon mustard

Pinch of ground nutmeg

SPECIAL TOOL

Pastry bag fitted with a ½-inch star tip

1. Preheat the oven to 400°F. Line 2 large rimmed baking sheets with parchment paper.

2. In a large saucepan, combine the water, milk, butter, and salt. Bring to a boil over medium-high heat. Immediately add the flour all at once, stirring vigorously with a wooden spoon. Continue to cook and stir until the mixture forms a ball. Remove from the heat and cool for 10 minutes.

3. Add the eggs, one at a time, beating vigorously after each addition until smooth. Stir in the cheese, mustard, and nutmeg.

4. Transfer the dough to a pastry bag fitted with a ½-inch star tip. Pipe the batter in 1-inch mounds close together on the prepared sheets.

5. Bake until puffed and golden, about 20 to 25 minutes. Serve warm.

JAGGED STONE'S SEAFOOD APPETIZERS

Ladybug here, popping in to share a couple of my very favorite recipes! We all know how important seafood is in the French culinary scene; from oysters to the catch of the day, aquatic-based options form a staple of our diet. But when the City of Light was threatened by the akumatized Kung Food, one simple seafood dish took on a decidedly dangerous twist. This recipe serves as a dedication to our all-time favorite, genuine rock 'n' roller Jagged Stone, whose duplicitous delivery of seafood appetizers deserves not one, but *two* namesake dishes. Shrimp Scampi Skewers are marinated in olive oil, lemon juice, and a pinch of red pepper, then dusted with finely grated Parmesan cheese. They're served alongside Tiny Tuna Tarts—cheesy, tasty tuna melts baked inside fresh and flaky puff pastry. Rich, savory, and undeniably delicious, Jagged Stone's Seafood Appetizers make for the perfect pairing. Just be sure to leave the villains at home . . . or send them packing, like Cat Noir and I aim to do! —*Ladybug*

SHRIMP SCAMPI SKEWERS

YIELD: 8 SERVINGS • GF

¼ cup olive oil

3 tablespoons fresh lemon juice

1 teaspoon lemon zest

2 large cloves garlic, minced

1 tablespoon chopped fresh curly-leaf parsley, plus more for garnish

Pinch of crushed red pepper

1¼ pounds large shrimp, peeled and deveined

4 tablespoons salted butter

2 tablespoons grated Parmesan cheese

Salt

SPECIAL TOOL

8 skewers

1. Prepare a grill for medium heat.
2. In a large bowl, whisk together the olive oil, lemon juice and zest, half of the garlic, parsley, and crushed red pepper. Add the shrimp and toss to coat. Cover and marinate in the refrigerator for 20 minutes. (Do not marinate any longer or the shrimp will start to break down.)
3. Drain the shrimp, discarding marinade. Thread the shrimp onto 8 skewers, leaving ¼ inch of space between them.
4. Grill until the shrimp are pink, 4 to 6 minutes, turning once halfway through grilling. Transfer to a serving platter.
5. While the shrimp are grilling, combine the butter and remaining minced garlic in a small saucepan. Heat over medium-low heat just until the butter is melted and the garlic is fragrant (do not burn).
6. Drizzle the shrimp with the garlic butter. Sprinkle with the Parmesan cheese, additional parsley, and salt to taste.

TINY TUNA TARTS

YIELD: 24 TARTS

⅓ cup mayonnaise

1 tablespoon finely chopped fresh parsley

1 tablespoon finely chopped fresh chives, plus more for garnish

1 tablespoon finely chopped fresh tarragon or basil

1 teaspoon lemon zest

2 teaspoons fresh lemon juice

1 teaspoon Dijon mustard

Freshly ground black pepper

Two 5-ounce cans white albacore tuna in olive oil, drained and flaked

1 cup shredded white cheddar cheese

Nonstick cooking spray

Half 17.3-ounce box frozen puff pastry (1 sheet), thawed

1. Preheat the oven to 375°F.

2. In a medium bowl, combine the mayonnaise, parsley, chives, tarragon, lemon zest and juice, mustard, and black pepper to taste. Stir until well blended. Stir in the tuna, breaking up large pieces with a fork. Stir in the cheese until well combined.

3. Spray two 12-cup mini muffin pans with cooking spray. On a lightly floured surface, roll out the puff pastry into a 10-by-15-inch rectangle. Cut the pastry into twenty-four 2½-inch squares. Press the squares into the prepared pans and prick with a fork.

4. Divide the tuna mixture evenly among the pastry cups. Bake until the pastry is puffed and the corners are golden brown, 14 to 16 minutes. Transfer to a serving platter. Sprinkle with additional fresh chives. Serve hot.

CHOCOLATE MILK MIX

YIELD: ABOUT 24 SERVINGS • V, GF

Breakfast is the most important meal of the day—though it should be noted that some of our favorite breakfast foods, from croissants to pain au chocolat, can be served at *any* time! And just like our treasured treats, this chocolate milk mix is the perfect beverage to start—or end—the day on a happy note. You can buy prepared chocolate milk mix, but we think making your own is fun and super easy! Just whisk with cold milk until frothy and you're good to go! Pair with a pastry—or one of Tikki's Favorite Chocolate Chip Cookies with Fleur de Sel (page 57)—and you'll have a positively perfect breakfast or after-school snack. Cheers! —*Marinette*

1 cup unsweetened cocoa powder

⅔ cup powdered sugar

2 tablespoons heavy cream powder

1. In a glass jar or container with a lid, combine the cocoa powder, powdered sugar, and heavy cream powder. Cover tightly and shake until well combined.

2. To make chocolate milk, whisk together 1½ cups cold milk (any kind) with a heaping tablespoon of the powder until smooth.

LE GRAND PARIS SIPPERS

YIELD: 4 DRINKS PER VARIATION • V, V+, GF

Our city is known for its elegant cafés and charming boulangeries, brasseries, and patisseries. But perhaps its most luxurious hangout is Le Grand Paris—the elegant hotel whose extraordinary restaurant is headed by our friend Alya's mother! Marlena's establishment makes the most delicious sippers, so of course we had to include our family's take on her signature fruity drinks. Le Grand Paris Sippers combine chilled sparkling water with mango, guava, or lime to create a trifecta of mocktails that pair perfectly with a side of scintillating conversation. Santé! —*Sabine*

MANGO-CITRUS FIZZ

Crushed ice

1 cup mango nectar

¾ cup fresh orange juice

3 tablespoons fresh lime juice

3 tablespoons mango syrup

1 cup soda water or sparkling water, chilled

4 thin slices fresh mango or orange twist, for garnish

GUAVA-LEMON SIPPER

Ice cubes

1½ cups guava nectar

¼ cup fresh lemon juice

3 tablespoons guava syrup

1 cup lemon-lime sparkling water, chilled

4 thin lemon slices, for garnish

LIME RICKEY–STYLE MOCKTAIL

Ice cubes

8 fresh mint leaves

1 cup fresh lime juice

½ cup simple syrup

2 tablespoons lime syrup

1⅓ cups ginger ale, chilled

4 lime wedges, for garnish

1. **To make the mango-citrus fizz:** Fill 4 rocks glasses with ice. In a 4-cup glass measuring cup or small pitcher, combine the nectar, juices, and syrup. Divide among the glasses; top each with ¼ cup of sparkling water and stir. Garnish with a slice of mango.

2. **To make the guava-lemon sipper:** Fill 4 Collins glasses with ice. In a 2-cup glass measuring cup, stir together the nectar, juice, and syrup. Divide among the glasses; top each with ½ cup of sparkling water and stir. Float a lemon slice on top.

3. **To make the lime rickey–style mocktail:** Fill 4 highball glasses with ice. Add the mint to a 2-cup glass measuring cup and gently bruise it with a muddler or the back of a spoon. Add the juice and syrups; stir. Divide among the glasses; top each with ⅓ cup of ginger ale and stir. Garnish with a lime wedge.

5
FROMAGE (CHEESE) FOR PLAGG

Bonjour from Cat Noir! When Ladybug told me that I could share some of my favorite cheesy dishes for the Dupain-Chengs' cookbook, my excitement was bubbling—just like a fresh pot of fondue! After all, my good friend Plagg absolutely adores a fine selection of cheeses, and I've learned it's in everyone's best interest to keep him happy. When I told him about this cookbook, he insisted that I provide the Dupain-Chengs with his absolute favorite cheesy dishes, so if you're a fellow turophile (that's fancy-speak for lover of all things cheese), read on. And prepare to be dazzled! —*Cat Noir*

PLAGG'S NEVER-BORED CHEESE BOARD

YIELD: 4 TO 6 SERVINGS • V

My close friend Plagg is a cheese-loving fiend with a strong affinity for Camembert. On more than one occasion, I've offered a chunk of his favorite fromage in exchange for his help in getting me out of a tricky situation! And when Plagg goes above and beyond to defuse a villainous situation, I show my thanks by making him this tasty, easy (and cheesy!) treat. Plagg's Never-Bored Cheese Board combines a collection of classic French cheeses—from hard cheeses like Comté, Mimolette, or Cantal, to soft cheeses like Morbier or Délice du Jura. Add some Brie, Camembert, or a pungent bleu cheese, and garnish with fresh fruits, jams, and nuts. Then serve alongside an array of crackers and baguette slices for a Plagg-perfect platter. Quelle fromage! —*Cat Noir*

3 ounces hard aged cheese (mature Comté, Mimolette, or Cantal)

3 ounces semisoft cheese (Morbier, Délice du Jura, or Tomme de Savoie)

3 ounces soft cheese (Brie, Camembert, or soft goat cheese)

3 ounces blue cheese (Roquefort, Bleu d'Auvergne, or Fourme d'Ambert)

Fruits (grapes, apples, pears, blackberries, dried apricots)

Nuts (almonds, walnuts, pistachios)

Sweet element (fig jam, cherry jam, honey)

Tom and Sabine Boulangerie Baguette (page 12), sliced, and/or lavash crackers

SPECIAL TOOL

Cheese plane or cheese knife, for hard cheeses

1. Arrange one type of cheese in each quadrant of a large cheese board or cutting board and fill in with the fruits, nuts, sweet element, and baguette slices. Place a cheese plane or cheese knife next to the hard cheese. Place a separate small knife next to the remaining cheeses.

CAMEMBERT CROQUE MONSIEUR

YIELD: 2 SANDWICHES

Plagg was insistent that I share his favorite recipe for France's famed sandwich, the croque monsieur. It's certainly among the most popular dishes at Parisian cafés, and Plagg's preferred recipe has adopted a decidedly delectable twist—one he finds to be délicieux! This version of the classic Parisian plate piles Camembert, ham, and Dijon mustard between slices of crusty white bread. Add a touch of grated Gruyère cheese sauce, and you're sure to have all the Parisians clamoring for a place at your table—including me and Plagg! —*Cat Noir*

GRUYÉRE CHEESE SAUCE

¾ cup whole milk

1 tablespoon unsalted butter

1 tablespoon all-purpose flour

½ cup grated Gruyère cheese, divided

¼ teaspoon kosher salt

⅛ teaspoon white pepper

⅛ teaspoon ground nutmeg

SANDWICHES

Four ½-inch-thick slices firm white bread, such as sourdough or ciabatta

1 tablespoon unsalted butter

4 thin slices Camembert

4 thin slices smoked ham

2 tablespoons Dijon mustard

1. Arrange an oven rack about 8 inches from the heat source. Preheat the oven to broil.

2. **To make the Gruyère cheese sauce:** In a small saucepan over medium heat, heat the milk until steaming (do not scorch). Remove from the heat. In another small saucepan over medium heat, melt the butter; decrease the heat to low. Add the flour and cook, whisking constantly, until golden, about 1 to 2 minutes. Gradually add the warm milk, whisking constantly until thickened, about 2 to 3 minutes. Remove from the heat. Gradually add ¼ cup of the Gruyère cheese; whisk until melted. Whisk in the salt, white pepper, and nutmeg.

3. **To make the sandwiches:** Heat a large skillet over medium-high heat. Spread one side of the bread slices with the butter. Place the bread, buttered side down, in the skillet and toast until golden, about 3 to 4 minutes. Transfer the bread to a work surface, toasted side down. Spread 2 tablespoons of the cheese sauce on 2 bread slices; add 2 slices of Camembert and 2 slices of ham. Spread the remaining 2 bread slices with mustard; place on top of the ham, mustard side down. Spread the remaining cheese sauce on top of the sandwiches; sprinkle with the remaining ¼ cup of Gruyère cheese.

4. Transfer the sandwiches to a rimmed baking sheet. Broil until the top is golden brown and bubbly, about 5 minutes.

MACARONI AU FROMAGE (MACARONI AND CHEESE)

YIELD: 6 TO 8 SERVINGS • V

The French know the importance of comfort food. And, as Plagg would say, what's more comforting than a cheesy baked pasta dish? Whether Ladybug and I have spent the day scouring the city for threats or de-akumatizing a fellow Parisian, we both appreciate the soothing power of a shared meal—preferably one that requires *loads* of different cheeses! Plagg's favorite homemade macaroni recipe calls on no fewer than three such fromages—grated Gruyère or Swiss, Roquefort or other blue cheese, and that timeless topper, mozzarella—blended with crème fraîche or sour cream to create an incredibly indulgent dish. Topped with seasoned breadcrumbs (and more cheese!) and baked to a bubbly goodness, this Macaroni au Fromage is sure to ease your troubles and erase any worries, one bite at a time. —*Cat Noir*

- ½ cup + 2 tablespoons salted butter, plus more for greasing
- 12 ounces cavatappi or macaroni pasta
- 2 cups freshly grated Gruyère or Swiss cheese
- 2 cups freshly grated low-moisture mozzarella cheese
- 1 cup Roquefort or other blue cheese crumbles
- ½ cup all-purpose flour
- ¼ teaspoon ground nutmeg
- ⅛ teaspoon ground white pepper
- 3 cups whole milk, warmed (100° to 110°F)
- ½ cup crème fraîche or sour cream
- 1½ cups soft, fresh breadcrumbs
- Snipped fresh chives or chopped fresh parsley for garnish

1. Preheat the oven to 350°F. Butter a 3-quart gratin or casserole dish. Cook the pasta according to the package directions.

2. In a medium bowl, toss together the Gruyère, mozzarella, and Roquefort cheeses. Reserve 1½ cups of the cheese mixture for the topping.

3. While the pasta is cooking, melt ½ cup of the butter in a large pot over low heat. Whisk in the flour, nutmeg, and white pepper. Gradually whisk in the milk and crème fraîche. Raise the heat to medium and cook, whisking constantly, until the mixture is thickened and bubbly. Remove from the heat. Stir in the larger portion of mixed cheeses and the hot cooked pasta, tossing to coat. Spoon into the prepared baking dish. Top with the reserved cheese mixture.

4. In a microwave-safe bowl, melt the remaining 2 tablespoons of butter; add the breadcrumbs and toss to coat. Sprinkle over the cheese. Bake until bubbly and golden brown, about 35 to 40 minutes. Let stand for 5 minutes before serving.

SOUPE À L'OIGNON GRATINÉE (FRENCH ONION SOUP)

YIELD: 6 SERVINGS

Another well-loved comfort food, Plagg's simplified recipe for French Onion Soup blends beef stock (prepared or homemade) with buttery caramelized onions. Top it off with a crusty, sliced baguette and a sprinkling of Gruyère and Parmesan cheeses to create a formidably flavorful dish that could warm Plagg's belly—and the heart!—on even the coldest winter's day. Bon appétit! —*Cat Noir*

- 4 tablespoons salted butter
- 6 medium yellow onions, halved and thinly sliced (about 6 cups)
- 4 cloves garlic, smashed
- 7 cups beef stock or broth
- 1 tablespoon red wine vinegar
- 3 sprigs fresh thyme, plus additional leaves for garnish
- Kosher salt
- Freshly ground black pepper
- Six ¾- to 1-inch-thick slices Tom and Sabine Boulangerie Baguette (page 12)
- ¾ cup shredded Gruyère or Swiss cheese
- ¼ cup + 2 tablespoons grated Parmesan cheese

1. In a large pot over medium heat, melt the butter. Add the onions and garlic. Cook, uncovered, until tender and lightly browned, 30 to 35 minutes, stirring occasionally. Add the broth, vinegar, and thyme sprigs. Bring to a boil. Decrease the heat and simmer, uncovered, for 20 to 26 minutes. Season to taste with salt and pepper.

2. Preheat the oven to broil. Arrange the bread slices on a baking sheet. Broil until lightly browned, 1 to 2 minutes per side, watching carefully to avoid burning. Sprinkle the bread slices with ½ cup of the Gruyère and ¼ cup of the Parmesan cheeses. Broil until the cheese is melted and golden, about 2 minutes, watching carefully to avoid burning.

3. Divide the soup among 6 crocks or bowls. Sprinkle the soup with the remaining ¼ cup of Gruyère and 2 tablespoons of Parmesan. Top each bowl with a toasted-cheese bread slice. Garnish with fresh thyme leaves.

FROMAGE GRILLÉ ET SOUPE À LA TOMATE (GRILLED CHEESE AND TOMATO SOUP)

YIELD: 4 SERVINGS • V

Children the world over love grilled cheese with tomato soup. (Of course, Plagg really enjoys the grilled cheese and not so much the soup.) He prefers his Fromage Grillé with artisan bread and authentically French cheeses, such as Brie or Camembert. I think it's best served with a homemade tomato soup—and a hearty side of conversation—making Fromage Grillé et Soupe à la Tomate a dish that's destined to bring friends and families together, one meal at a time. —*Cat Noir*

SOUP

4 tablespoons unsalted butter

1 medium sweet onion, diced

¼ cup tomato paste

One 28-ounce can whole tomatoes

2 cups water

½ cup heavy whipping cream, plus more for serving

½ teaspoon kosher salt

Snipped fresh basil, for garnish

SANDWICHES

8 slices sourdough or artisan bread

2 tablespoons butter, at room temperature

2 tablespoons Dijon mustard

8 ounces sliced French cheese, such as Gruyère, Camembert, Brie, or Swiss Emmental

SPECIAL TOOL

Immersion blender or blender

1. **To make the soup:** In a medium pot over medium heat, melt the butter. Add the onion and cook, stirring frequently, until translucent, 3 to 4 minutes. Add the tomato paste and cook, stirring constantly, until fragrant, about 1 minute.

2. Stir in the tomatoes along with their juice and the water. Use a wooden spoon to break up the tomatoes. Bring to a boil, then decrease the heat to low and simmer until the liquid has reduced slightly, about 10 minutes. Use an immersion blender to blend until very smooth. (Or blend in batches in a regular blender, returning all the soup to the pot.) Stir in the heavy whipping cream and reheat gently over low heat. Stir in the salt. Keep warm over low heat.

3. **To make the sandwiches:** Lightly spread one side of the bread slices with the butter. Spread the other side of the bread slices with the mustard. Top 4 of the mustard sides of the bread slices with cheese. Top with the remaining 4 bread slices, mustard sides down, buttered sides up.

4. Heat a large skillet over medium heat. Place the sandwiches in the skillet and cook until the bread is golden and the cheese is melted, 5 to 6 minutes, turning once halfway through cooking.

5. Ladle the soup into bowls. Drizzle with heavy cream and top with snipped fresh basil. Serve with the sandwiches.

TARTIFLETTE

YIELD: 4 TO 6 SERVINGS • GF

When the weather turns cold, Plagg likes to turn to warm, hearty dishes filled with rich ingredients and packed with savory flavors—like a tasty tartiflette. This alpine casserole combines potatoes and onions with garlic, bacon, fresh thyme, crème fraîche, and a generous helping of Plagg's favorite soft cheeses. C'est délicieux! —*Cat Noir*

Salted butter, at room temperature, for buttering the baking dish

2 pounds Yukon Gold potatoes, peeled and sliced ½ inch thick

8 ounces thick-cut or slab bacon, cut into ¼-inch dice (lardons)

2 medium yellow onions, halved and sliced

2 cloves garlic, minced

1 teaspoon finely chopped fresh thyme

Pinch of ground nutmeg

¾ cup chicken broth

2 tablespoons white wine vinegar

Kosher salt

Freshly ground black pepper

½ cup heavy cream

12 ounces soft cow's milk cheese, such as Délice du Jura, Brie, or Camembert, cut into ½-inch slabs (leave the rind on)

1. Preheat the oven to 400°F. Butter a 2-quart gratin or casserole dish.

2. Bring a large pot of lightly salted water to a boil over high heat. Add the potatoes and cook at a low boil until a fork can be inserted into the center of a slice but the potatoes aren't mushy, about 12 to 15 minutes. (They should be fully cooked but not overcooked.) Drain the potatoes and set aside.

3. Place the bacon in a large cold skillet over medium heat. Cook the bacon until some of the fat renders and the edges are golden but the bacon is not crisped, about 7 to 8 minutes. Remove the bacon to a paper towel–lined plate to drain. Remove all but about 2 teaspoons of the bacon fat in the pan.

4. Add the onion, garlic, thyme, and nutmeg to the pan and cook, stirring frequently, until the onions are translucent, about 5 to 7 minutes. Add the chicken broth and white wine vinegar, scraping with a wooden spoon to release any flavorful browned bits from the bottom of the pan.

5. Arrange half of the potatoes in the prepared baking dish. Season lightly with salt and pepper. Arrange half of the onion mixture and half of the bacon over the potatoes. Top with the remaining potatoes. Season lightly with salt and pepper. Top with the remaining onion mixture and bacon. Drizzle with the heavy cream.

6. Arrange the cheese slices on top of the casserole. Bake in the middle of the oven until bubbling and the cheese is melted and lightly browned, about 30 to 40 minutes. Let stand for 5 minutes before serving.

6
SOUPES ET SALADES
(SOUPS AND SALADS)

Paris is known for many things—its bread, its art, and occasionally, its overcast days. When the clouds creep over the city, we like to indulge in a hearty helping of soup—a dish that warms the heart every bit as much as it nourishes the body. The recipes in this section offer cheerful nods to our most beloved family recipes, French staples, and even the hero herself, Ladybug! Soup and salad is a perfect pairing, and these recipes are sure to leave our family and friends with a smile. —*Sabine*

SPECIAL-POWERS SEAWEED SOUP

YIELD: 4 SERVINGS • GF

Cat Noir and I have a very special friend—one who just happens to possess extraordinary powers. While I can't reveal too much about him, let's just say that I can always turn to him whenever I need a little boost. Special-Powers Seaweed Soup is our heroes' tribute to the grimoire's aquatic spell. Prepared with dashi, tofu, and wakame, along with a branch from the dragon king's garden (or as the Parisians call it, seaweed!), this oceanic delicacy is a healthy blend that's brimming with flavor. Serve alongside crispy roasted seaweed (if you like!), and this soup is sure to imbue anyone who slurps it with the powers of the sea. Spoons—and tridents!—up! —*Ladybug*

¼ cup white miso

4 cups hot prepared instant dashi, made according to package directions

8 ounces silken tofu

1 tablespoon wakame flakes

2 scallions, very thinly sliced

Roasted seaweed snack, for serving (optional)

1. Place the miso in a small bowl. Add a ladleful of the hot dashi to the miso. Stir with a small spoon until the miso is completely dissolved, breaking up any lumps if necessary. Add the miso mixture to the pot of dashi. Keep the dashi hot but do not let it boil.

2. Drain off excess liquid from the tofu. Gently place it on a cutting board. Carefully cut it into ½-inch dice. Add to the pot. Add the wakame flakes and scallions to the pot. Stir gently to combine the ingredients.

3. Divide among 4 bowls and serve hot.

MARINETTE SOUP

YIELD: 4 SERVINGS • GF

My great-uncle, Wang Cheng Sifu, is a super-famous Chinese chef. His Celestial Soup is legendary—for more reasons than one. After he entered a cooking competition at Le Grand Paris, his soup was compromised and my uncle was akumatized into the villain Kung Food! But once he was back to himself, he taught me how to create his well-balanced sweet potato soup. Using chicken broth, garlic, coriander, and the petals of the purple pansies I gave him as a welcome gift, he renamed his renowned dish Marinette Soup, and with it, went on to win the title of World's Greatest Chef! This recipe recreates his famous delicacy, crafting an Asian flavor profile with sesame oil, ginger, and optional Thai chile. It's topped off with a swirl of curry-carrot cream and a purple pansy. Sweet and surprisingly savory—with a hit of heat—Marinette Soup is a tasty tribute to my incredible uncle . . . and it tastes très bon, too! —*Marinette*

SOUP

1 tablespoon olive oil

1 large yellow onion, chopped

1½ pounds purple sweet potatoes, peeled and roughly chopped

1 small apple, peeled, cored, and chopped

1 Thai chile pepper, seeded and chopped (optional)

3 cloves garlic, minced

1 tablespoon minced fresh ginger

1 teaspoon ground coriander

1 teaspoon kosher salt

½ teaspoon black pepper

4 cups chicken broth, plus more as needed

1 tablespoon apple cider vinegar

CURRY-CARROT CREAM

1 large carrot, chopped

1 tablespoon water

One 6-ounce can coconut cream

1 teaspoon curry powder

⅛ teaspoon kosher salt

GARNISH

Edible pansies

SPECIAL TOOL

Immersion blender

1. **To make the soup:** In a large saucepan over medium heat, heat the oil. Add the onion and cook until tender, stirring occasionally, about 4 to 5 minutes. Add the sweet potatoes and apple; cook until they begin to soften, stirring occasionally, about 8 to 10 minutes. Add the chile pepper (if using), garlic, and ginger; cook for 30 seconds. Add the coriander, salt, and black pepper. Add the broth and vinegar. Bring to a boil over medium-high heat. Simmer, covered, until the potatoes are tender, about 20 minutes.

2. **To make the curry-carrot cream:** Meanwhile, add the carrot and water to a small microwave-safe bowl. Cover with plastic wrap, venting one corner. Cook on high for 3 minutes. Let stand for 1 minute. Test with a fork; if it's not very tender, cook on high for 1 minute longer. Transfer the carrot to a small bowl; add the coconut cream, curry powder, and salt. Use an immersion blender to blend until smooth.

3. Let the soup cool slightly. Use an immersion blender* to blend until smooth. If the soup is too thick, add more broth, ¼ cup at a time, until the desired consistency is reached.

    *****Tip:** *Or carefully transfer the soup to a high-speed blender, in batches if necessary, and blend until smooth.*

4. Top each serving with a swirl of the curry-carrot cream and garnish with an edible pansy.

VICHYSSOISE
(POTATO-LEEK SOUP)

YIELD: 6 TO 8 SERVINGS • GF

A few years after French-born Louis Diat became the head chef of the Ritz-Carlton Hotel in New York City in 1911, he fancied up the humble potato-leek soup his mother used to make to create this elegant soup that is now a staple of Parisian cuisine. Other than its velvety, light creaminess and delicate flavor, the most notable thing about vichyssoise is that it can be served chilled when it's hot outside or hot when it's cold. Vichyssoisse is a classic French soup that will be every bit as popular at your dinner table as it is in our home. —*Sabine*

2 large leeks, halved horizontally and sliced (white and light green parts only)

2 tablespoons salted butter

½ teaspoon kosher salt

2 cloves garlic, minced

1 pound russet potatoes, peeled and diced*

4 cups chicken broth

1 bay leaf

1 cup heavy cream

½ cup buttermilk

Ground white pepper

Snipped fresh chives for garnish

SPECIAL TOOL

Blender

1. Place the sliced leeks in a bowl of cool water and swirl to remove grit and dirt. Drain and repeat. Pat dry with a clean paper towel.

2. In a large saucepan or soup pot over medium heat, melt the butter. Add the leeks and salt. Decrease the heat to low and cook, stirring frequently, until the leeks are very tender but not browned, about 10 to 15 minutes. Add the garlic and cook just until it is fragrant, 1 minute. Add the potatoes, chicken broth, and bay leaf. Bring to a boil over high heat. Decrease the heat, cover, and simmer until the potatoes are very tender, about 15 to 20 minutes. Remove from the heat and let cool for a few minutes.

   Tip: *Peel and cut the potatoes just before using so they don't turn brown to keep your soup a beautiful creamy white.*

3. Remove the bay leaf and discard. Blend the mixture in batches in a blender until very smooth. Return to the pot.

4. Stir in the cream and buttermilk. Season to taste with additional salt, if necessary, and ground white pepper to taste.

5. To serve warm, reheat as necessary and ladle into bowls. Garnish with fresh chives.

6. To serve cold, let stand until room temperature, then transfer to a container with a tightly sealed lid and chill in in the refrigerator for at least 4 hours. Garnish with fresh chives just before serving.

SALADE PARISIENNE

YIELD: 2 SERVINGS • GF

This classic Parisian creation is proof that salad can be hearty. Buttery, tender baby Boston lettuce leaves are tossed with a very French mustard-shallot vinaigrette, then topped with boiled Yukon Gold potatoes, quartered hard-boiled eggs, cubed ham, and Emmental cheese. Our family's Salade Parisienne is a filling and flavorful dish that we come back to every summer . . . and winter, too! Quelle délice! —*Tom*

- 4 cups mixed tender greens (mâche, arugula, frisée, baby spinach, torn Bibb or Boston lettuce)
- ¼ cup Mustard-Shallot Vinaigrette (page 100), plus more to taste
- 2 medium Yukon Gold potatoes, cooked, cooled, and cubed
- 2 hard-boiled eggs, quartered
- 3 ounces thick-sliced ham, diced
- 3 ounces semihard cheese (Gruyère, Comté, or Swiss Emmental), diced
- 4 cornichons, chopped
- Kosher salt
- Freshly ground black pepper
- Snipped fresh chives for garnish

1. In a medium bowl, toss the greens with the vinaigrette. Divide between 2 serving plates.
2. Top the dressed greens with the potatoes, eggs, ham, cheese, and cornichons. Season to taste with salt and black pepper. Garnish with chives. Serve with additional vinaigrette.

FRENCH BISTRO SALAD

YIELD: 4 SERVINGS • V

A handful of dishes can be found at any proper French bistro—steak frites, croque monsieur, and of course, a wholesome array of fresh garden vegetables. No proper eatery would be complete without offering a generous serving of the latter—preferably mixed into a delightfully crisp salad! The French Bistro Salad is our family's take on this classic dish. Crisp, mixed greens are tossed in a homemade mustard-shallot vinaigrette and topped with slices of baked goat cheese. Served with a sliced baguette, this popular salad makes for a magnifique meal. —*Tom*

SALAD

1 head butterhead (Bibb or Boston) lettuce

2 heads Little Gem (baby romaine) lettuce

¾ cup panko breadcrumbs

¾ teaspoon dried thyme

One 8-ounce log goat cheese, cut into 8 equal pieces

¼ cup extra-virgin olive oil

4 small radishes, trimmed and thinly sliced

Kosher salt

Freshly ground black pepper

GARLIC TOASTS

Twelve ¼-inch-thick slices day-old Tom and Sabine Boulangerie Baguette (page 12)

2 tablespoons extra-virgin olive oil

1 large clove garlic, halved

MUSTARD-SHALLOT VINAIGRETTE

1 tablespoon minced shallot

3 tablespoons white wine vinegar

Kosher salt

Freshly ground black pepper

½ cup extra-virgin olive oil

1 tablespoon Dijon mustard

2 teaspoons minced fresh chives

SPECIAL TOOL

Salad spinner

1. **To make the salad:** Trim the ends of the butterhead and Little Gem lettuces. Separate the leaves. Place in a salad spinner. Fill with cold water. Add a couple of handfuls of ice cubes and swirl around with your hand. Let stand for 5 minutes.

2. Drain and spin the lettuces as dry as possible. Place in the refrigerator to chill while you prepare the remaining ingredients.

3. **To make the garlic toasts:** Preheat the oven to 350°F.

4. Brush both sides of the bread slices with olive oil. Arrange on a large rimmed baking sheet. Bake until golden brown, about 15 minutes, turning halfway through the baking time. Immediately rub both sides of the toasts with the cut sides of the garlic. Set aside.

5. **To make the vinaigrette:** In a small jar with a lid, combine the shallot, vinegar, and salt and pepper to taste. Let stand for 5 minutes to allow the shallot to soften slightly. Add the oil, mustard, and chives. Cover tightly and shake vigorously until blended and emulsified. Set aside.

6. Increase the oven to 400°F. Lightly oil a large rimmed baking sheet.

7. In a shallow bowl or plate, combine the breadcrumbs and dried thyme. Slightly flatten the goat cheese slices and form into disks. Brush both sides of the cheese disks with the olive oil. Coat both sides in the seasoned breadcrumbs. Arrange on the prepared baking sheet. Bake until golden brown and bubbly, 10 to 12 minutes.

8. Meanwhile, tear the lettuces into bite-size pieces and place in a large bowl. Add the radishes and toss to combine. Shake the vinaigrette to recombine, if necessary. Add about ½ cup of the vinaigrette to the bowl and toss to coat. Taste and add more vinaigrette, or salt and pepper, if necessary. (You want it flavorful but lightly dressed.)

9. To serve, divide the salad among 4 plates. Top each with 2 slices of the baked goat cheese. Place 3 garlic toasts on the side of each plate. Serve immediately.

7
ENTRÉES

The literal meat and potatoes (or more accurately, Cordon Bleu and Quiche) of our family meals, these entrées feature prominently at the Dupain-Cheng dining table. We're incredibly excited to feature recipes from Ladybug and Cat Noir alongside our personal family favorites—a heroic addition to some already super options. From pizza to soufflé, our entrées have earned rave reviews from family, friends, and superheroes alike. —*Tom*

SABINE'S CHICKEN CORDON BLEU WITH HERB-BUTTER PEAS

YIELD: 4 SERVINGS

Our family is the very heart of my world. Not only do I love helping Tom develop breads, pastries, and sweets for the Boulangerie, but I absolutely adore creating homemade meals to fuel my husband and my daughter's creativity. Classic Chicken Cordon Bleu ("blue ribbon chicken") is one of Marinette's favorites. It may sound fancy and hard to make, but it's really just chicken breast cutlets stuffed with one of our favorite cheeses (we're partial to Gruyère or Swiss) and ham, breaded and pan-fried until crispy, then finished in the oven. Draped with creamy herbed Dijonnaise and served with a side of mixed peas and carrots tossed in parsley-dill butter, it's a marvelous meal—whether you serve it at a family dinner or repurpose it for a lunchtime treat. —*Sabine*

HERBED DIJONNAISE

⅓ cup mayonnaise

⅓ cup crème fraîche or sour cream

¼ cup chopped herbs (such as chives, tarragon, and parsley)

¼ cup buttermilk

3 tablespoons Dijon mustard

Salt

Freshly ground black pepper

CHICKEN

Two 8-ounce boneless, skinless chicken breasts

Kosher salt

Freshly ground black pepper

4 slices Gruyère or Swiss cheese, each cut into 3 strips

4 slices Black Forest ham

1½ cups panko breadcrumbs

¼ cup grated Parmesan cheese

½ teaspoon garlic powder

½ cup all-purpose flour

1 large egg, beaten

Neutral oil (such as canola or grapeseed) for frying

1. **To make the herbed Dijonnaise:** In a medium bowl, whisk together the mayonnaise, crème fraîche, chopped herbs, buttermilk, Dijon mustard, and salt and black pepper to taste. Cover and refrigerate until ready to serve.

2. **To make the chicken:** Preheat the oven to 350°F. Place an oven-safe wire rack on a large rimmed baking sheet; set aside.

3. Place a chicken breast on a clean work surface. Press down firmly on top with your hand. Carefully cut the breast in half to make two thin cutlets. Place each half between two pieces of plastic wrap and use a meat mallet or rolling pin to gently pound it to an even ¼-inch thickness. Repeat with the remaining chicken breast.

4. Place the chicken cutlets, smooth side down, on the work surface. Season with salt and pepper. Arrange 3 strips of cheese crosswise in the center of each cutlet. Top each with a slice of ham. Fold each cutlet into thirds, like a letter, over the ham and cheese to seal; secure with wooden toothpicks.

5. In a wide, shallow bowl, whisk together the breadcrumbs, Parmesan cheese, garlic powder, and salt and pepper to taste. Place the flour and the egg in 2 separate wide, shallow bowls. Dredge a chicken piece in the flour, shaking off the excess. Dip in the egg, letting the excess drip off. Dredge in the breadcrumb mixture to evenly coat. Place on the prepared rack. Repeat with the remaining chicken pieces.

6. Pour ¼ inch of oil into a large skillet; heat over medium heat. Working in 2 batches, place the chicken in the hot oil and fry until golden brown, about 3 to 4 minutes per side. Return to the prepared rack.

ingredients and recipe continued on next page

continued from previous page

PEAS

½ cup matchstick-cut carrots

2½ cups sugar snap peas, trimmed and strings removed

1½ cups fresh or frozen English peas

3 tablespoons salted butter

2 teaspoons minced fresh parsley

1 teaspoon chopped fresh dill

½ teaspoon kosher salt

SPECIAL TOOL

Instant-read thermometer

7. Transfer the baking sheet and rack to the oven and bake until the chicken is cooked through, about 15 to 20 minutes, or until the interior reaches 165°F. Remove from the oven and tent with foil to keep warm.

8. **To make the peas:** Bring a large pot of salted water to a boil over high heat. Add the carrots and return to a boil; cook for 1 minute. Add the sugar snap peas and English peas. When the water returns to a boil, cook for 3 minutes. Drain and return the vegetables to the pot. Add the butter, parsley, dill, and salt, stirring until well coated.

9. Serve the chicken with the peas and Dijonnaise.

KUNG FOOD'S PEPPERONI PIZZA SWORD

YIELD: 4 SERVINGS

When Cheng Sifu was akumatized into the villainous chef Kung Food, his frightening alter ego came after me and Cat Noir! His pepperoni pizza sword was rumored to be absolutely deadly—definitely *not* the tasty treat Marinette, Alya, and their friends at Collège Françoise Dupont frequently enjoy! Kung Food's Pepperoni Pizza Sword is my cheeky nod to Cheng Sifu's culinary weapon—one that was super scary at the time, but that I'm able to laugh about now. I make my (*non*-dangerous!) food-based weapon with homemade pizza dough, which I shape into a sword and top with fresh sauce. Once I top it with shredded mozzarella and loads of pepperoni, it magically morphs into the *best* snack. No villains required! —*Ladybug*

CRUST

1 cup warm water (105° to 115°F)

1 tablespoon honey

1 package (2¼ teaspoons) instant yeast or active dry yeast

2¾ cups bread flour or all-purpose flour, plus more for kneading

¾ teaspoon kosher salt

3 tablespoons olive oil

PIZZA SAUCE

1 tablespoon olive oil

½ cup finely chopped onion

2 cloves garlic, minced

One 8-ounce can tomato sauce

½ teaspoon dried oregano

½ teaspoon dried basil

¼ teaspoon kosher salt

¼ teaspoon black pepper

¼ teaspoon crushed red pepper

PIZZA

2 cups shredded mozzarella

One 5-ounce package mini pepperoni

SPECIAL TOOLS

Two 13-by-18-inch baking sheets

1. **To make the crust:** Line two 13-by-18-inch baking sheets with parchment paper; set aside.

2. In a large bowl, whisk together the water, honey, and yeast. Let stand until foamy, about 5 minutes.

3. In a medium bowl, whisk together the flour and salt. Add the olive oil to the yeast mixture. Using a wooden spoon, gradually stir in 2 cups of the flour to the yeast mixture. Stir in the remaining ¾ cup of flour.

4. Turn the dough out onto a lightly floured surface. Knead until the dough is smooth and bounces back when poked with a finger, adding more flour as necessary to keep the dough from sticking, about 5 to 6 minutes.

5. Place the dough in a lightly greased bowl. Cover and let rise in a warm place until doubled in size, about 1 hour.

6. **Meanwhile, to make the pizza sauce:** In a small saucepan over medium heat, heat the oil. Add the onion and cook, stirring occasionally, until tender, 3 to 5 minutes. Add the garlic and cook for 30 seconds. Stir in the tomato sauce, oregano, basil, salt, black pepper, and crushed red pepper. Bring to a simmer and cook, uncovered, until slightly thickened, about 5 minutes.

7. Punch down the dough and turn it out onto a lightly floured surface. Divide the dough into 2 equal portions. Working with one portion at a time, roll the dough into a 5-by-13-inch rectangle, with the long side running parallel to the edge of your work surface. Starting at the lower left corner of the rectangle, use a sharp knife or pizza cutter to cut a rounded blade shape, ending in a point at the upper right corner. The sword blade should be about two-thirds of the rectangle, with one-third of the dough remaining. Transfer the

continued on next page

continued from previous page

sword-blade portion to one of the prepared baking sheets, adjusting the shape, if necessary.

8. Divide the remaining one-third of the dough into 2 portions, one about one-third of the remaining dough and the other about two-thirds. Roll and shape the larger portion into an 6-by-2-inch rectangle to create the guard. Place the long edge next to the wide side of the sword blade, leaving about ¼ inch in between. Roll and shape the smaller portion into a 3-by-1-inch rectangle and place a short end next to the guard, leaving about ¼ inch in between, to create the grip. If necessary, use the parchment to rotate the pizza sword diagonally across the pan to fit. Repeat with the remaining dough portion and second prepared baking sheet. Lightly cover and let rise until lightly puffed, about 30 minutes.

9. **To make the pizza:** Preheat the oven to 400°F.

10. Top the blade portion of each sword with half of the pizza sauce, 1 cup of the cheese, and half of the pepperoni slices.

11. Bake until the crust is golden brown and the cheese is bubbling, 10 to 12 minutes, rotating the pans between racks halfway through the baking time. Let stand for 5 minutes before serving.

Note: *To simplify this recipe, use purchased pizza sauce and a 1-pound package of refrigerated prepared pizza dough. Let the dough sit at room temperature for 1 hour before using.*

CHEESE-AND-VEGETABLE PESTO PIZZA

YIELD: 2 TO 4 SERVINGS • V

My grandfather Roland is old-fashioned. He owns a '72 Le Panyol—a super rare wood-fired oven—and he didn't leave his home for over twenty years! Since he wasn't exactly welcoming to visitors, I snuck into his house disguised as the flour delivery person. There I promptly discovered that Grandfather isn't just anti-travel, he's anti-pizza, too! Even though he considers it sacrilegious to put cheese and vegetables on bread, I happen to like pizza. And I *really* like this particular recipe! When it's my turn to cook family dinners, I add pesto, mozzarella, and an array of fresh vegetables—from cherry tomatoes to mini bell peppers—to a round of homemade dough. Cheese-and-Vegetable Pesto Pizza is fresh, flavorful, and fun enough to get a smile out of even the most reclusive relatives. Bon appétit, Papy! —*Marinette*

CRUST

¾ cup warm water (105° to 115°F)

1 teaspoon granulated sugar

Half 0.25-ounce package active dry yeast (1⅛ teaspoons)

2 cups all-purpose flour, plus more for rolling

½ teaspoon kosher salt

2 tablespoons olive oil

Cornmeal for dusting

TOPPINGS

3 tablespoons olive oil

One 8-ounce package cremini mushrooms, sliced

4 red, orange, and/or yellow mini bell peppers, cored and sliced

2 cloves garlic, minced

½ teaspoon kosher salt

2 cups cherry tomatoes

3 tablespoons pesto

6 ounces fresh mozzarella, sliced ¼ inch thick, then halved

½ cup quartered black olives

SPECIAL TOOL

Electric mixer

1. **To make the crust:** In a small bowl, stir together the water, sugar, and yeast. Let stand until the yeast is foamy, about 5 minutes.

2. In a large bowl, stir together the flour and salt. Add the yeast mixture and olive oil. Beat with an electric mixer on medium speed until the dough forms a ball, about 4 to 5 minutes. Turn the dough out onto a lightly floured surface; knead to form a smooth ball that is firm and elastic.

   Tip: *If the dough is too dry, add water, 1 teaspoon at a time, until the dough comes together. If the dough is too wet, add flour, 1 tablespoon at a time, until the desired consistency is reached.*

3. Lightly oil a large bowl; add the dough and turn to coat. Cover with plastic wrap and let rise until doubled in size, about 1 hour.

4. Preheat the oven to 450°F. Lightly oil a large baking sheet.

5. **Meanwhile, to make the toppings:** In a large skillet over medium heat, heat 1 tablespoon of the oil. Add the mushrooms and bell peppers and cook, stirring occasionally, until the mushrooms are golden and the peppers are crisp-tender, about 4 to 5 minutes. Add the garlic and salt; cook for 30 seconds. Transfer to a bowl or plate.

6. Add the remaining 2 tablespoons of oil to the skillet and heat over medium-high heat. Add the tomatoes and cook undisturbed for 2 minutes to blister the bottoms. Cook, stirring occasionally, until the tomatoes begin to shrivel, about 2 to 3 minutes.

7. Punch down the dough and turn it out onto a lightly floured surface. Use floured hands or a rolling pin to press the dough into a 12-inch circle. Transfer to the prepared baking sheet. Use a fork to prick holes in the dough. Bake for 5 minutes, then remove from the oven.

8. Spread the pesto over the crust to within ½ inch of the edge. Top with the cheese. Add the mushroom-pepper mixture, tomatoes, and olives. Bake until the cheese is bubbly and the crust is golden brown, about 6 to 8 minutes.

   Note: *To simplify this recipe, substitute 1 pound of purchased pizza dough. Let the dough sit at room temperature for 1 hour before using.*

UNCLE WANG'S STEAMED DUMPLINGS

YIELD: 40 DUMPLINGS

As a chef, Uncle Wang has plenty of specialty dishes. His dumplings are favorites in my family—and they're sure to become a classic in your own home, too. The mixture is placed in prepared dumpling wrappers, then folded by hand, as is the traditional way. From our family to yours, these steamed dumplings are sure to become a treasured tradition.
—*Sabine*

3 ounces dried shiitake mushrooms

8 ounces ground pork

4 ounces large shrimp, peeled, deveined, and minced

3 tablespoons minced water chestnuts

1 scallion, trimmed and minced

1 teaspoon minced fresh ginger

1 clove garlic, minced

1 tablespoon oyster sauce

1 teaspoon toasted sesame oil

¼ teaspoon kosher salt

⅛ teaspoon ground white pepper

½ teaspoon granulated sugar

1 large egg white, beaten

Forty 3-inch siu mai (dumpling) wrappers

Finely minced carrot, if assembling by hand

Cabbage leaves for steaming (optional)

Soy sauce, for serving

SPECIAL TOOLS

Dumpling press (optional)

Steamer basket

1. Rinse the dried mushrooms under cool running water. Place in a small bowl and add warm water to cover. Soak for 20 to 30 minutes or until softened; drain. Remove stems and discard. Mince the caps.

2. In a large bowl, combine mushroom caps, pork, shrimp, water chestnuts, scallion, ginger, garlic, oyster sauce, sesame oil, salt, pepper, sugar, and egg white. Stir vigorously to combine and create a paste-like texture. Cover and chill in the refrigerator for 4 hours.

3. To assemble the dumplings, hold a wrapper flat on one hand. Place about 2 teaspoons of the filling in the center of the wrapper. Use the back of a spoon to pack the filling in tightly. Bring the wrapper up around the filling, pressing lightly to adhere it to the filling while gently rotating to create "pleats" around the edge. Lightly squeeze the dumpling around the middle to keep the filling intact during steaming. Gently tap bottom of dumpling on the counter to flatten so it will stand upright. Top with a little minced carrot. Repeat with the remaining wrappers and filling, covering the wrappers with a damp towel to keep them from drying out as you work.

4. **Alternatively, use a dumpling press:** Place a wrapper on top of the press. Place about 2 teaspoons of filling on one half of the wrapper, leaving a border for sealing. Moisten the edge of the empty half with a little bit of water. Close the dumpling press to seal. Repeat with the remaining filling and wrappers. You will not use the carrot in this method.

5. Line a steamer basket with cabbage leaves or parchment that has several small holes poked in it to keep the dumplings from sticking. Fill the bottom of the pot with water, being careful that it comes close to but doesn't touch the bottom of the basket. Place just enough dumplings in the basket so that there is at least ½ inch between them. (Dumplings will stick to each other if they touch.) Bring the water to a boil, then add the basket to the pot. Cover and steam until the filling is cooked through, 5 to 8 minutes. Repeat with the remaining dumplings, adding more water as necessary.

6. Serve with soy sauce.

UNCLE WANG'S SHANGHAI-STYLE NOODLES

YIELD: 4 SERVINGS

My mom was *thrilled* when I offered to deliver Uncle Wang's birthday present to Shanghai. She'd always wanted me to visit the place where she'd grown up, and my trip meant my uncle's gift would actually arrive on time! We celebrated at his Thousand Delights restaurant, where I learned that on your birthday, a special longevity tradition requires that the celebrant try to slurp the longest noodle possible without breaking it. Inspired by Uncle Wang's incredible dishes, Shanghai-Style Noodles are made with thick udon noodles that are stir-fried with meat or tofu, shiitake mushrooms, and baby bok choy. They're tossed with a soy-sesame sauce and drizzled with chili oil, making this a healthful, well-seasoned dish to serve at *any* celebratory meal. —Marinette

MARINADE

2 tablespoons light soy sauce

1 tablespoon rice wine vinegar

1 teaspoon cornstarch

12 ounces boneless pork, thinly sliced; skinless boneless chicken breasts or thighs, thinly sliced; or firm tofu, cubed

SAUCE

¼ cup chicken broth

2 tablespoons light soy sauce

1 tablespoon dark soy sauce

2 teaspoons brown sugar

1 teaspoon sesame oil

1 teaspoon cornstarch

¼ teaspoon ground white pepper

STIR-FRY

1 pound udon noodles

2 tablespoons vegetable oil

6 shiitake mushrooms, stemmed, caps sliced

½ cup coarsely grated carrot

2 scallions, cut diagonally into 2-inch pieces

3 baby bok choy, cut into ribbons

Chili oil (optional)

1. **To make the marinade:** In a medium bowl, stir together the soy sauce, vinegar, and cornstarch. Add the meat and stir to coat; let stand while preparing the sauce and vegetables.

2. **To make the sauce:** In a small bowl, whisk together the broth, soy sauces, brown sugar, sesame oil, cornstarch, and white pepper. Set aside.

3. **To make the stir-fry:** Bring a large pot of water to a boil over high heat, add the noodles, and cook for 1 minute. Drain.

4. In a large skillet or wok over medium-high heat, heat 1 tablespoon of the oil. Add the meat; cook golden brown, 2 to 3 minutes. Transfer to a bowl. Add the remaining 1 tablespoon of oil to the skillet. Add the mushrooms, carrot, and scallions; cook until the mushrooms have softened, about 3 to 4 minutes. Add the meat, noodles, bok choy, and sauce. Using tongs to toss the stir-fry, cook until the sauce has thickened, the noodles are coated, and the bok choy has wilted, about 2 to 3 minutes. Lightly drizzle with chili oil, if using.

SABINE'S SALMON AND SPINACH QUICHE

YIELD: 6 SERVINGS

When Marinette's friends join us at our home, we make sure to have a variety of foods on hand. After all, the way to a teenager's heart is definitely through their stomach! My Salmon and Spinach Quiche is a healthful, protein-rich treat that makes for a delightful after-school snack . . . especially when preparing for the Paris Ultimate Mecha Strike III Tournament! To keep it simple, prepared piecrust is filled with a custardy mixture of eggs, smoked salmon, baby spinach, and fresh goat cheese. Topped with fresh chives, and served warm from the oven, this savory pie draws friends to the table for a spot of sprightly conversation. C'est délicieux! —*Sabine*

1 prepared piecrust, thawed if frozen

1 tablespoon salted butter

1 large shallot, minced

4 cups roughly chopped baby spinach

4 large eggs

1 cup heavy cream

½ cup whole milk

2 tablespoons minced fresh parsley

1 tablespoon minced fresh chives, plus more for garnish

Salt

Freshly ground black pepper

Pinch of ground nutmeg

6 ounces hot-smoked salmon, skin removed and broken into ½-inch pieces

¾ cup crumbled fresh goat cheese, divided

SPECIAL TOOL

10-inch quiche dish or tart pan with a removable bottom

1. Preheat the oven to 375°F.

2. Roll out the piecrust on a lightly floured surface to an 11-inch circle. Gently ease into a 10-inch quiche dish or tart pan with a removable bottom, pressing along the sides gently to adhere the crust to the dish.

3. In a large skillet over medium heat, melt the butter. Add the shallot and cook until softened, about 2 to 3 minutes. Add the spinach and cook just until wilted, about 1 to 2 minutes; set aside.

4. In a large bowl, whisk together the eggs, cream, milk, parsley, chives, salt and pepper to taste, and nutmeg. Remove the spinach from the pan with a slotted spoon and stir into the egg mixture. Gently stir in the salmon and ½ cup of the goat cheese.

5. Transfer the mixture to the prepared pan. Sprinkle the remaining ¼ cup of cheese on top. Bake until the crust is golden brown and the center is set, about 25 minutes. Let stand for 5 minutes before serving. Sprinkle with fresh chives.

COLOMBO DE POULET

YIELD: 6 SERVINGS • GF

Our family isn't the only culinarily minded family in town. Alya Césaire's mom is the head chef of Le Grand Paris hotel, which means mealtimes at her house are *never* boring! One of her most impressive dishes is Colombo de Poulet, a Caribbean-style curry loaded with amazing flavor from so many spices! After Marlena made it for Marinette, we recreated the recipe—and we're excited to share it with you. Chicken and two kinds of potatoes (Yukon Gold and sweet) are braised in a mixture of freshly ground spices and coconut milk. Zucchini is added at the end of cooking so it doesn't get mushy! Serve over rice to create a meal that's every bit as amazing as the Césaire family. Mes compliments au chef! —*Sabine*

1 recipe Seed Mixture (recipe follows)

3 pounds meaty chicken pieces (breast halves, thighs, and drumsticks), skin removed, larger pieces cut in half

2 tablespoons olive oil

Kosher salt

Freshly ground black pepper

1 medium red onion, thinly sliced

4 cloves garlic, minced

1 teaspoon chopped serrano chile pepper

½ cup chicken broth

One 14-ounce can coconut milk

3 tablespoons fresh lime juice

2 tablespoons Colombo Powder (recipe follows)

½ to 1 teaspoon crushed red pepper

3 Yukon Gold potatoes, peeled and cut into quarters

1 medium sweet potato, peeled and cubed

1 zucchini, peeled and sliced into half-moons

Cooked white rice, for serving

SPECIAL TOOLS

Mortar and pestle

Blender or food processor

Instant-read thermometer

1. Rub the seed mixture all over the chicken. In a Dutch oven over medium heat, heat the oil. Brown the chicken, in batches if necessary, for about 4 minutes on each side. Season with salt and black pepper. Transfer to a plate.

2. In the same pan, cook the onion until tender, 4 to 5 minutes. Add the garlic and serrano; cook for 1 minute. Add the broth; scrape up the browned bits from the bottom of the pan. Add the coconut milk, lime juice, Colombo Powder, and crushed red pepper. Stir. Return the chicken to the pan; add the potatoes. Season with salt and black pepper.

3. Simmer, covered, stirring occasionally, for about 45 minutes. Add the zucchini. Stir to combine. Cook, uncovered, until an instant-read thermometer registers 165°F when inserted into the chicken, about 15 minutes longer. Serve with cooked rice.

Seed Mixture: In a mortar and pestle, coarsely grind ½ teaspoon coriander seeds, ½ teaspoon brown mustard seeds, ½ teaspoon cumin seeds, and ½ teaspoon fenugreek seeds.

Colombo Powder: In a medium skillet over medium heat, toast ¼ cup white rice, stirring occasionally, until lightly golden, about 5 minutes. Transfer to a plate to cool. Add ¼ cup cumin seeds, ¼ cup coriander seeds, 1 tablespoon brown mustard seeds, 1 tablespoon black peppercorns, 1 tablespoon fenugreek seeds, and 1 teaspoon whole cloves to the skillet. Toast over medium heat until fragrant, stirring frequently, about 3 minutes. Add to the plate to cool. Add the rice and spices to a blender or food processor. Process to a fine powder; transfer to a bowl. Stir in ¼ cup ground turmeric. Store in an airtight container for up to 6 months.

HOT DOG DAN'S MAGICAL HOT HOGS

YIELD: 4 SERVINGS

On a class trip to New York City, we learned about a *really* unique American superhero. Hot Dog Dan lives in "The Big Apple," where he sells magical hot dogs that temporarily grant the diner superpowers. These dogs have given Dan's patrons glowing skin, magic hair, and even the ability to float. Although this particular recipe doesn't *technically* grant heroic abilities, it does tend to leave people feeling pretty darned super after eating it. Hot Dog Dan's Magical Hot Dogs take classic New York sausages and pile them high with spicy brown mustard, sauerkraut, and homemade onion sauce. Toss in some jalapeños and who knows—fire breathing might just be in the cards after all! —*Marinette*

ONION SAUCE

2 tablespoons vegetable oil

2 medium onions, thinly sliced

½ cup water

¼ cup ketchup

1 tablespoon brown sugar

1 teaspoon hot sauce

½ teaspoon mild chili powder

½ teaspoon kosher salt

¼ teaspoon black pepper

¼ teaspoon ground cinnamon

HOT DOGS

4 all-beef hot dogs

4 hot dog buns, split

1 cup sauerkraut

Spicy brown mustard

Thinly sliced jalapeños (optional)

1. **To make the onion sauce:** In a large skillet over medium heat, heat the oil. Add the onions and cook, stirring occasionally, until golden, 8 to 10 minutes. Stir in the water, ketchup, brown sugar, hot sauce, chili powder, salt, black pepper, and cinnamon. Bring to a boil; lower the heat and simmer, uncovered, until thickened, about 10 minutes. Transfer the sauce to a bowl; cool to room temperature before serving. (The sauce can be made up to 2 days ahead.)

2. **To make the hot dogs:** Bring a large saucepan of water to a boil over medium-high heat. Add the hot dogs. Boil, uncovered, until the hot dogs are plump, 4 to 6 minutes. Remove with tongs and drain on a paper towel–lined plate.

3. Place the hot dogs in the buns; add some of the onion sauce and the sauerkraut. Top with mustard and sliced jalapeños, if you like.

VINCENT'S SPAGHETTI

YIELD: 4 SERVINGS

My friend Adrien is the most awesome of awesome models. His radiant face is on billboards all over Paris! Alya and I often see him out and about shooting with his photographer, Vincent. (We just happen to be passing by—of course!) After hearing the famed photographer used spaghetti to elicit a variety of absolutely adorable emotions from Adrien, I was inspired to make this dish. Vincent's Spaghetti offers a tiny twist on the classic dish—spaghetti tossed with a simple, Italian-style marinara sauce and the *cutest* mini meatballs. It's a recipe that's easy to make and bound to be popular with kids, parents, and teenage models alike! —*Marinette*

MINI MEATBALLS

¼ cup plain breadcrumbs

⅓ cup milk

1 egg, beaten

2 tablespoons minced onion

1 clove garlic, minced

2 tablespoons minced fresh parsley

½ teaspoon Italian seasoning

¼ teaspoon crushed red pepper

½ teaspoon fennel seeds

½ teaspoon kosher salt

¼ teaspoon black pepper

8 ounces ground beef

8 ounces ground pork

MARINARA SAUCE

2 tablespoons olive oil

2 cloves garlic, minced

One 28-ounce can crushed tomatoes (preferably San Marzano)

½ teaspoon kosher salt

¼ teaspoon black pepper

⅛ teaspoon crushed red pepper

2 tablespoons snipped fresh basil

Pinch of granulated sugar (optional)

12 ounces dried spaghetti (preferably bronze-cut)

¼ cup grated Parmigiano Reggiano

Fresh basil leaves for garnish

1. **To make the meatballs:** Preheat the oven to 400°F. Line a large rimmed baking sheet with parchment paper.

2. In a large bowl, combine the breadcrumbs and milk. Let stand for 15 minutes.

3. Add the egg, onion, garlic, parsley, Italian seasoning, crushed red pepper, fennel seeds, salt, and black pepper. Stir until combined. Add the ground beef and pork and mix gently with your hands until well combined.

4. Shape the mixture into thirty-two ¾-inch meatballs. Place the meatballs on the prepared baking sheet. Bake until browned and cooked through, about 15 to 20 minutes; drain off the fat.

5. **To make the marinara:** In a large saucepan over medium heat, heat the oil. Add the garlic and cook just until fragrant, 30 seconds to 1 minute. Add the tomatoes, salt, black pepper, crushed red pepper, and basil. Bring to a boil, then decrease the heat and simmer until slightly thickened, about 15 to 20 minutes. Add a pinch of sugar, if desired.

6. Add the cooked meatballs to the marinara and keep warm.

7. Cook the spaghetti according to the package directions, reserving ¼ cup of the cooking water. Drain.

8. Toss the cooked spaghetti with the meatballs and sauce, adding a splash of the reserved pasta cooking water, if necessary, to loosen the sauce.

9. Divide the spaghetti and meatballs among 4 shallow bowls. Sprinkle with Parmigiano Reggiano cheese and garnish with a basil leaf.

CAT NOIR'S MASHED POTATOES AND SAUSAGE

YIELD: 4 SERVINGS • GF

During Cheng Sifu's akumatization, I squared off against the momentarily malevolent Mayor Bourgeois. The mayor came at me with a string of potatoes and sausages, but I wasn't impressed—as I told him, I prefer my sausages with *mashed* potatoes! After that eventful showdown, I went home and enjoyed a dish inspired by my opponent's unlikely weapon . . . and of course, I had to share the recipe with you! To make Cat Noir's Mashed Potatoes and Sausage, I sear fresh garlic pork sausages and serve them with garlic mashed potatoes topped with a creamy onion sauce and snipped fresh chives. They're a hero-worthy dish that my friend Plagg says could only be better with a hearty chunk of Camembert. (He thinks *everything* is better with Camembert!) —*Cat Noir*

POTATOES

1½ pounds russet potatoes, peeled and quartered

Kosher salt

2 tablespoons butter

¼ cup whole milk, warmed (100° to 110°F), plus more as needed

Freshly ground black pepper

Snipped fresh chives for garnish

FRENCH ONION SAUCE

1 tablespoon salted butter

1 medium yellow onion, thinly sliced

1 cup heavy cream

¼ teaspoon kosher salt, plus more to taste

⅛ teaspoon ground white pepper

Pinch of ground nutmeg

SAUSAGES

4 garlic pork sausages or bratwurst

1 tablespoon olive oil

SPECIAL TOOLS

Blender

Fine-mesh strainer

1. **To make the potatoes:** Bring a medium saucepan of salted water to a boil over high heat. Add the potatoes and cook, covered, until tender, 20 to 25 minutes.

2. **To make the onion sauce:** While the potatoes are cooking, melt the butter in a small saucepan over medium. Add the onion and cook, stirring frequently, until softened but not browned and most of the liquid has evaporated, about 20 minutes.

3. Stir in the cream. Heat just until bubbles start to form, about 2 minutes. Simmer over medium-low heat for about 5 minutes. Transfer to a blender. Start blending on low speed, then gradually increase the speed to high and blend until a smooth sauce forms, about 1 minute. Pour the sauce through a fine-mesh strainer set over the saucepan. Stir in the salt, white pepper, and nutmeg. Taste and adjust the seasonings if needed. Keep warm over very low heat, stirring occasionally, until ready to serve.

4. **To make the sausages:** Place sausages in a medium saucepan and cover with cold water. Place over medium-high heat and cook just until the water begins to simmer, 6 to 8 minutes. Remove from the pan and pat dry with paper towels.

5. While the sausages cook, drain the potatoes and return them to the pan. Add the butter and warm milk. Mash with a potato masher, adding more milk to achieve the desired consistency. Season to taste with salt and black pepper. Keep warm until serving time.

6. To finish the sausages, heat the olive oil in a large saucepan over medium-high heat. Add the cooked sausages and brown in the oil until crisp-skinned, turning occasionally, 4 to 5 minutes.

7. To serve, place 1 sausage on each of 4 dinner plates. Divide the mashed potatoes among the plates. Make a small well in each pile of mashed potatoes. Top the potatoes with the onion sauce and garnish with snipped fresh chives.

TOM'S SUPERHERO BRUNCH

As a protective papa, I'll do anything to take care of my family—whether it's waking up early to bake at our Boulangerie Patisserie or protecting my pastries from an akumatized baby villain that happens to be obsessed with cake! Thankfully, when that towering, tempestuous toddler arrived on the scene I didn't have to fight him off alone—Cat Noir jumped right in! For his impressive efforts in protecting our city—and for always making sure to look out for our bakery—our family owes Cat Noir our eternal gratitude. And since we tend to show appreciation through food, I was honored to cook the hero a multicourse brunch—one he and Marinette eagerly tucked into.

The meal began with Sweetheart Vol-Au-Vents—heart-shaped puff pastry shells filled with creamed chicken and wild mushrooms. That was followed by my Simple Cheese Soufflé, which puffs up to incredible heights without having to separate the eggs and beat the whites separately—which is the traditional method for making soufflé. (That's why it's simple!). Made with love and (optionally) baked in the shape of a heart, these dishes are bound to be popular items at your own family brunch—so long as it's served with lots of love! —*Tom*

SWEETHEART VOL-AU-VENTS WITH WILD MUSHROOM–CHICKEN FILLING

YIELD: 6 SERVINGS

EGG WASH

1 large egg

1 tablespoon water

PUFF PASTRY SHELLS

Half 17.3-ounce box frozen puff pastry (1 sheet), thawed, well chilled

SAUCE

3 tablespoons unsalted butter

3 tablespoons all-purpose flour

¼ cup chicken broth

1 cup heavy cream or crème fraîche

¼ teaspoon kosher salt

¼ teaspoon black pepper

1. Preheat the oven to 400°F. Line a rimmed baking sheet with parchment paper.

2. **To make the egg wash:** In a small bowl, whisk together the egg and water. Set aside.

3. **To make the puff pastry shells:** On a lightly floured surface, roll out the pastry to ¼ inch thick. Use a 3-inch heart-shaped cutter to cut out 12 hearts; place 6 of the hearts on the baking sheet (these are the bottoms). For the tops, use a 2-inch heart-shaped cutter to partially cut a smaller heart out of the 6 remaining larger hearts (do not cut all the way through the pastry). Place the tops on the bottoms. Bake until the pastry is puffed and golden, about 20 minutes. Let cool.

4. **To make the sauce:** Meanwhile, in a medium saucepan over medium heat, melt the butter and then whisk in the flour. In a 2-cup glass measuring cup, stir together the broth and cream. Whisk the cream mixture into the flour-butter mixture until smooth. Season with salt and pepper. Cook, stirring constantly, until the mixture is thickened. Remove from the heat.

ingredients and recipe continued on next page

continued from previous page

FILLING

1 tablespoon unsalted butter

8 ounces mixed wild mushrooms, finely chopped

2 cloves garlic, minced

2 teaspoons finely chopped parsley

¼ teaspoon kosher salt

¼ teaspoon black pepper

1 cup diced cooked chicken

SPECIAL TOOLS

3-inch heart-shaped cookie cutter

2-inch heart-shaped cookie cutter

5. **To make the filling:** In a large skillet over medium heat, melt the butter. Add the mushrooms and cook until golden brown, about 5 to 6 minutes. Add the garlic, parsley, salt, and pepper; cook for 1 minute. Add the chicken and heat through. Stir the filling into the sauce; cook until heated through, about 2 minutes.

6. Use a sharp knife to carefully lift the small heart from the top of the pastry. Spoon the mushroom-chicken sauce into the cavity of each pastry. Place the small pastry heart on top.

SIMPLE CHEESE SOUFFLÉ

YIELD: 4 SERVINGS • V

6 tablespoons butter, plus more for greasing

1 tablespoon finely grated Parmesan cheese

6 tablespoons all-purpose flour

2 cups whole milk, warmed (100° to 110°F)

¾ teaspoon kosher salt

¼ teaspoon ground white pepper

Pinch of ground nutmeg

1 teaspoon Dijon mustard

5 large eggs

2 cups + 1 tablespoon shredded Gruyère or Comté cheese

2 tablespoons minced fresh chives

1 tablespoon panko breadcrumbs

SPECIAL TOOL

6-cup heart-shaped or regular soufflé dish

1. Preheat the oven to 400°F. Butter a 6-cup heart-shaped or regular soufflé dish. Coat the bottom and sides evenly with the Parmesan cheese; set aside.

2. In a medium saucepan over medium heat, melt the butter. Whisk in the flour until well combined. Cook for 10 seconds, whisking constantly, then whisk in the milk. Cook, whisking constantly, until the mixture comes to a boil and begins to thicken and become smooth, about 3 to 5 minutes. Remove from the heat. Whisk in the salt, white pepper, nutmeg, and mustard. Set aside to cool for 10 minutes.

3. While the milk mixture is cooling, whisk the eggs in a medium bowl until smooth. Gradually whisk the beaten eggs, 2 cups of the cheese, and the chives into the milk mixture until smooth and well combined. Pour the mixture into the prepared soufflé dish. Sprinkle the remaining 1 tablespoon Gruyère cheese and the breadcrumbs over the top.

4. Bake until puffy and browned, about 25 to 30 minutes. Serve immediately.

8
GLACES
(ICE CREAMS)

André Glacier, the sweetheart matchmaker, serves his glaces with a side of romance. It's said that couples who eat his ice cream will stay in love forever—something I hope is true, since my parents got engaged while enjoying some of André's culinary creations!

To André, crafting creamy concoctions is more than a job—it's his passion! He's spent years dreaming up unique flavors at home, hoping to enchant his daily life by creating an especially sweet treat. When he realized his true calling was to enchant other people's lives by sharing his delightful recipes, his business was born, and Parisians have been flocking to him ever since. André was kind enough to share some of his recipes with us, and we proudly include them for you to make at home. (You know, on days you don't have three hours to spare to go find his cart!) After all, there's very little that can't be solved by a generous serving of ice cream—preferably one composed of two scoops that have been paired to perfection! —*Marinette*

ANDRÉ GLACIER'S ICE CREAMS

YIELD: EIGHT ½-CUP SERVINGS PER VARIATION • V, GF

Each of the following recipes can be served alone or combined with another flavor to create an utterly exquisite pairing. May love (and love of ice cream!) never end!

ICE CREAM BASE

2 cups heavy cream

1 cup whole milk

1 cup granulated sugar

1 teaspoon vanilla extract

⅛ teaspoon fine sea salt

SPECIAL TOOLS

1- to 2-quart ice-cream maker

Food processor or blender

Fine-mesh strainer

1. Place the ice cream-maker bowl in the freezer at least 12 hours before making ice cream.

2. **To make the ice cream base:** In a medium saucepan, heat the cream, milk, sugar, vanilla, and salt over medium-low heat, stirring frequently, until the sugar is dissolved and the mixture is warm, about 3 to 4 minutes. Pour into a bowl. Cover and chill for at least 2 hours or overnight. Whisk the base, then pour it into the ice-cream maker bowl.

3. Churn according to the manufacturer's directions. Transfer the ice cream to a 1-quart container and freeze for at least 2 hours to ripen.

Blueberry Ice Cream: In a medium saucepan over medium heat, cook 1 pint fresh blueberries and the 1 cup granulated sugar used in the Ice Cream Base, stirring frequently, until the berries soften and burst open, about 10 minutes. Cook until mixture is jammy,

continued on next page

continued from previous page

5 to 10 minutes longer. Let cool for 15 minutes. Stir the cream, milk, vanilla, and salt into the berry mixture. Chill, covered, until completely cooled, at least 1 hour or up to overnight. Pour into the ice-cream maker and proceed with the directions above.

Lemon Ice Cream: Add ⅓ cup fresh lemon juice and 1 tablespoon grated lemon zest to the Ice Cream Base just before chilling.

Mint Ice Cream: Add about 20 fresh mint leaves to the saucepan along with the cream when making the Ice Cream Base. After heating, let stand for 10 minutes. Strain the mint leaves. Proceed with the directions above.

Peach Ice Cream: In a medium bowl, combine 2 cups peeled chopped fresh peaches with ½ cup of the sugar used in the Ice Cream Base; let stand for 15 minutes for the fruit to release its juice. In a food processor or blender, puree the peaches. Add the cream, milk, remaining ½ cup sugar, vanilla, and salt to the saucepan and proceed with the Ice Cream Base. Add the pureed peaches to the base before chilling. Pour into the ice-cream maker and proceed with the directions above.

Peppermint Ice Cream: Add 1 cup crushed candy canes and 1 teaspoon peppermint extract to the chilled Ice Cream Base. Top servings with crushed candy canes.

continued on next page

continued from previous page

Pistachio Ice Cream: Add 1 cup coarsely chopped roasted and lightly salted pistachios, 1 drop green food coloring (optional), and 1 to 2 drops pistachio essence (optional) to the ice-cream maker after about 20 minutes of churning.

Strawberry and Blackberry Ice Creams: In a medium bowl, combine 1 pint strawberries or blackberries and ½ cup of the sugar used in the Ice Cream Base. Slightly mash the berries with a fork. Let stand for 15 minutes for the fruit to release its juice. In a food processor or blender, puree the berry mixture until smooth. Strain the seeds using a fine-mesh strainer; return the puree to the bowl. Add the cream, milk, remaining ½ cup sugar, vanilla, and salt to the saucepan, and proceed with the Ice Cream Base. Add the pureed berry mixture to the base before chilling. (For Blackberry Ice Cream, add ½ teaspoon grated lemon zest.) Pour into the ice-cream maker and proceed with the directions above.

Strawberry with Chocolate Chip Ice Cream: Prepare Strawberry Ice Cream, adding 4 ounces finely chopped semisweet chocolate to the ice-cream maker after about 20 minutes of churning.

Vanilla Bean Ice Cream: Use 1 vanilla bean, split lengthwise and seeded, in place of the vanilla extract in the Ice Cream Base.

Orange Sorbet: Do not use Ice Cream Base. In a medium saucepan over medium heat, add ¾ cup granulated sugar and ¼ cup water and cook, stirring frequently, until the sugar is dissolved. Remove from the heat. Add 3 cups fresh orange juice; stir until combined. Chill, covered, until completely cooled. Pour into the ice-cream maker and proceed with the directions above.

DIETARY CONSIDERATIONS

V = Vegetarian   V+ = Vegan   GF = Gluten free

Pains (Breads)

Tom and Sabine Boulangerie Baguettes V, V+

Pain d'Epi (Wheat Stalk Bread) V, V+

Roland's Ancient-Method Loaf V

Tom's Modern-Method Loaf V, V+

Multigrain Bâtard Rolls V

Brioche à Têtes V

Pâtisseries (Pastries)

Cat Noir's Chouquettes V

Tom's Tarte aux Fruits V

Ladybug Éclairs V

Galette de Rois (King's Cake) V

Tom and Sabine Patisserie Croissants V

Gateaux et Biscuits (Cakes and Cookies)

Candy Apple Cake Pops V

Pound It! Cake V

Eiffel Tower Cake V

Derby Hat Cake V

Marinette's Birthday Cake V

Birthday Cake for Adrien V

Bûche de Noël V

Tikki's Favorite Chocolate Chip
Cookies with Fleur de Sel V

Lucky Charm and Cataclysm Cupcakes V

Miraculous Macarons V, GF

Apéritifs, Collations, et Boissons (Appetizers, Snacks, and Beverages)

Ladybug Canapés V

Radishes with Herbed Butter and Salt V

Cheese Bombs V

Shrimp Scampi Skewers GF

Tiny Tuna Tarts

Chocolate Milk Mix V, GF

Le Grand Paris Sippers V, V+, GF

Fromage (Cheese) for Plagg

Plagg's Never-Bored Cheese Board V

Camembert Croque Monsieur

Macaroni au Fromage (Macaroni and Cheese) V

Soupe à l'Oignon Gratinée (French Onion Soup)

Fromage Grillé et Soupe à la Tomate
(Grilled Cheese and Tomato Soup) V

Tartiflette GF

Soupes et Salades (Soups and Salads)

Special-Powers Seaweed Soup GF

Marinette Soup GF

Vichyssoise(Potato-Leek Soup) GF

Salade Parisienne GF

French Bistro Salad V

Entrées

Sabine's Chicken Cordon Bleu with Herb-Butter Peas

Kung Food's Pepperoni Pizza Sword

Cheese-and-Vegetable Pesto Pizza V

Uncle Wang's Steamed Dumplings

Uncle Wang's Shanghai-Style Noodles

Sabine's Salmon and Spinach Quiche

Colombo de Poulet GF

Hot Dog Dan's Magical Hot Hogs

Vincent's Spaghetti

Cat Noir's Mashed Potatoes and Sausage GF

Sweetheart Vol-au-Vents with Wild
Mushroom–Chicken Filling

Simple Cheese Soufflé V

Glaces (Ice Creams)

André Glacier's Ice Creams V, GF

CONVERSION TABLES

KITCHEN MEASUREMENTS

CUP	TABLESPOON	TEASPOON	FLUID OUNCES
$^{1}/_{16}$ cup	1 tablespoon	3 teaspoons	½ fluid ounce
$^{1}/_{8}$ cup	2 tablespoons	6 teaspoons	1 fluid ounce
$^{1}/_{4}$ cup	4 tablespoons	12 teaspoons	2 fluid ounces
$^{1}/_{3}$ cup	$5^{1}/_{3}$ tablespoons	16 teaspoons	$2^{2}/_{3}$ fluid ounces
$^{1}/_{2}$ cup	8 tablespoons	24 teaspoons	4 fluid ounces
$^{2}/_{3}$ cup	$10^{2}/_{3}$ tablespoons	32 teaspoons	$5^{1}/_{3}$ fluid ounces
$^{3}/_{4}$ cup	12 tablespoons	36 teaspoons	6 fluid ounces
1 cup	16 tablespoons	48 teaspoons	8 fluid ounces

GALLON	QUART	PINT	CUP	FLUID OUNCES
$^{1}/_{16}$ gallon	$^{1}/_{4}$ quart	½ pint	1 cup	8 fluid ounces
$^{1}/_{8}$ gallon	½ quart	1 pint	2 cups	16 fluid ounces
$^{1}/_{4}$ gallon	1 quart	2 pints	4 cups	32 fluid ounces
½ gallon	2 quarts	4 pints	8 cups	64 fluid ounces
1 gallon	4 quarts	8 pints	16 cups	128 fluid ounces

OVEN TEMPERATURES

CELCIUS	FAHRENHEIT
93°C	200°F
107°C	225°F
121°C	250°F
135°C	275°F
149°C	300°F
163°C	325°F
177°C	350°F
191°C	375°F
204°C	400°F
218°C	425°F
232°C	450°F

WEIGHT

GRAMS	OUNCES
14 grams	½ ounce
28 grams	1 ounce
57 grams	2 ounces
85 grams	3 ounces
113 grams	4 ounces
142 grams	5 ounces
170 grams	6 ounce s
283 grams	10 ounces
397 grams	14 ounce
454 grams	16 ounces
907 grams	32 ounces

LENGTH

IMPERIAL	METRIC
1 inch	2½ centimeters
2 inches	5 centimeters
3 inches	$7^{2}/_{3}$ centimeters
4 inches	10 centimeters
6 inches	15 centimeters
8 inches	20 centimeters
12 inches	30 centimeters

ABOUT THE AUTHORS

Lisa Kingsley has more than thirty years' experience as a food writer, editor, and recipe developer. Her work has appeared in magazines such as *Fine Cooking* and *Better Homes & Gardens*. She collaborated with the Smithsonian Institution on *American Table: The Foods, People, and Innovations That Feed Us* (Harvest, 2023). She is the coauthor of *Cooking with Magic: A Century of Recipes Inspired by Disney's Animated Films from* Steamboat Willie *to* Wish (Insight Editions, 2023) and *The Powerpuff Girls: The Official Cookbook* (Insight Editions, 2024).

S. T. Bende is a young-adult and children's author, known for the Norse mythology series *Viking Academy* and the *Ære Saga*. She's also written books for Disney, Lucasfilm, Pixar, The Jim Henson Company, and Marvel. She lives on the West Coast, where she spends far too much time at Disneyland, and she dreams of skiing on Jotunheim and Hoth. www.stbende.com

ACKNOWLEDGEMENTS

LISA KINGSLEY   To all of the superhero home chefs and bakers who help save their corner of the world one grilled cheese sandwich—or bite of baguette—at a time.

S. T. BENDE   A huge thank you to the *miraculous* Insight team for always letting me play in my fandoms. And to Sami and Paul for shepherding this gorgeous book into the world. Merci beaucoup to the talented Lisa Kingsley, whose delectable recipes brought the Dupain-Cheng's world to life. And mille mercis to my ahh-mazing family for sharing so many fun-filled French adventures. (Eiffel Tower-adjacent lightsaber ice cream will forever be one of my favorite memories!) Your unparalleled sense of adventure is *simply the best!*

INDEX

A

Almond flour
King's Cake, 35
Miraculous Macarons, 61–62

B

Bacon
Tartiflette, 90
Baguettes, Tom and Sabine Boulangerie, 12
Beef
Hot Dog Dan's Magical Hot Hogs, 120
Vincent's Spaghetti, 121
Blackberry Ice Cream, 136
Bread
Brioche à Têtes, 23
Multigrain Bâtard Rolls, 20
Roland's Ancient-Method Loaf, 17–19
Tom and Sabine Boulangerie Baguettes, 12
Tom's Modern-Method Loaf, 19
Wheat Stalk Bread, 14–16
Brioche à Têtes, 23
Bûche de Noël, 53–55

C

Cakes
Birthday Cake for Adrien, 50–52
Bûche de Noël, 53–55
Candy Apple Cake Pops, 40
Derby Hat Cake, 45–47
Eiffel Tower Cake, 43–44
Lucky Charm and Cataclysm Cupcakes, 58
Marinette's Birthday Cake, 49
Pound It! Cake, 41
Canapés
Ladybug Canapés, 69

Radishes with Herbed Butter and Salt, 70
Candy Apple Cake Pops, 40
Carrots
Marinette Soup, 97
Sabine's Chicken Cordon Bleu with Herb-Butter Peas, 105–6
Uncle Wang's Shanghai-Style Noodles, 115
Cheese
Camembert Croque Monsieur, 84
Cheese-and-Vegetable Pesto Pizza, 110–11
Cheese Bombs, 71
French Bistro Salad, 100
French Onion Soup, 87
Grilled Cheese and Tomato Soup, 89
Kung Food's Pepperoni Pizza Sword, 107–9
Ladybug Canapés, 69
Macaroni and Cheese, 86
Plagg's Never-Bored Cheese Board, 83
Sabine's Chicken Cordon Bleu with Herb-Butter Peas, 105–6
Sabine's Salmon and Spinach Quiche, 116
Salade Parisienne, 99
Simple Cheese Soufflé, 129
Tartiflette, 90
Tiny Tuna Tarts, 74
Chicken
Colombo de Poulet, 119
Sabine's Chicken Cordon Bleu with Herb-Butter Peas, 105–6
Sweetheart Vol-au-Vents with Wild Mushroom–Chicken Filling, 125–26

Chocolate
Bûche de Noël, 53–55
Chocolate Milk Mix, 76
Ladybug Éclairs, 31–32
Strawberry with Chocolate Chip Ice Cream, 136
Tikki's Favorite Chocolate Chip Cookies with Fleur de Sel, 57
Chouquettes, Cat Noir's, 27
Colombo de Poulet, 119
Cookies
Miraculous Macarons, 61–62
Tikki's Favorite Chocolate Chip Cookies with Fleur de Sel, 57
Croissants, Tom and Sabine Patisserie, 36
Croque Monsieur, Camembert, 84
Cupcakes, Lucky Charm and Cataclysm, 58

D

Derby Hat Cake, 45–47
Drinks
Chocolate Milk Mix, 76
Guava-Lemon Sipper, 79
Lime Rickey–Style Mocktail, 79
Mango-Citrus Fizz, 79
Dumplings, Uncle Wang's Steamed, 112

E

Éclairs, Ladybug, 31–32
Eiffel Tower Cake, 43–44

F

French Bistro Salad, 100
French Onion Soup, 87
Fromage Grillé et Soupe à la Tomate, 89

Fruit. *See also specific fruits*
  Plagg's Never-Bored
    Cheese Board, 83
  Tom's Tarte aux Fruits, 28

G

Galette de Rois, 35
Greens
  French Bistro Salad, 100
  Sabine's Salmon and
    Spinach Quiche, 116
  Salade Parisienne, 99
Guava-Lemon Sipper, 79

H

Ham
  Camembert Croque Monsieur, 84
  Sabine's Chicken Cordon Bleu
    with Herb-Butter Peas, 105–6
  Salade Parisienne, 99
**Hot Hogs, Hot Dog
  Dan's Magical,** 120

I

Ice Cream Base, 132
Ice Creams, André Glacier's, 132–36

K

King's Cake, 35

L

Leek-Potato Soup, 98
Lemon
  Guava-Lemon Sipper, 79
  Lemon Ice Cream, 135
Lettuce
  French Bistro Salad, 100
  Salade Parisienne, 99
Lime Rickey–Style Mocktail, 79

M

Macaroni au Fromage, 86
Macarons, Miraculous, 61–62

Mango-Citrus Fizz, 79
Marinette Soup, 97
Marshmallows
  Derby Hat Cake, 45–47
  Eiffel Tower Cake, 43–44
Mint. *See also* **Peppermint**
  Lime Rickey–Style Mocktail, 79
  Mint Ice Cream, 135
Multigrain Bâtard Rolls, 20
Mushrooms
  Cheese-and-Vegetable
    Pesto Pizza, 110–11
  Sweetheart Vol-au-Vents
    with Wild Mushroom–
    Chicken Filling, 125–26
  Uncle Wang's Shanghai-
    Style Noodles, 115
Mustard-Shallot Vinaigrette, 100

N

**Noodles, Uncle Wang's
  Shanghai-Style,** 115
Nuts. *See also* **Almond flour**
  Pistachio Ice Cream, 136
  Plagg's Never-Bored
    Cheese Board, 83

O

Olives
  Cheese-and-Vegetable
    Pesto Pizza, 110–11
  Ladybug Canapés, 69
Onions
  Cat Noir's Mashed Potatoes
    and Sausage, 123
  French Onion Soup, 87
  Hot Dog Dan's Magical
    Hot Hogs, 120
  Tartiflette, 90
Orange
  Mango-Citrus Fizz, 79
  Orange Sherbet, 136

P

Pan d'Epi, 14–16
Passion fruit
  Birthday Cake for Adrien, 50–52
Pasta and noodles
  Macaroni and Cheese, 86
  Uncle Wang's Shanghai-
    Style Noodles, 115
  Vincent's Spaghetti, 121
Pastries
  Cat Noir's Chouquettes, 27
  Cheese Bombs, 71
  King's Cake, 35
  Ladybug Éclairs, 31–32
  Sweetheart Vol-au-Vents
    with Wild Mushroom–
    Chicken Filling, 125–26
  Tiny Tuna Tarts, 74
  Tom and Sabine Patisserie
    Croissants, 36
  Tom's Tarte aux Fruits, 28
Peach Ice Cream, 135
**Peas, Herb-Butter, Sabine's Chicken
  Cordon Bleu with,** 105–6
Peppermint
  Bûche de Noël, 53–55
  Peppermint Ice Cream, 135
**Pepperoni Pizza Sword,
  Kung Food's,** 107–9
Peppers
  Cheese-and-Vegetable
    Pesto Pizza, 110–11
**Pesto Pizza, Cheese-and-
  Vegetable,** 110–11
Pistachio Ice Cream, 136
Pizza
  Cheese-and-Vegetable
    Pesto Pizza, 110–11
  Kung Food's Pepperoni
    Pizza Sword, 107–9
Pork. *See also* **Ham**
  Cat Noir's Mashed Potatoes
    and Sausage, 123

Kung Food's Pepperoni
  Pizza Sword, 107–9
Tartiflette, 90
Uncle Wang's Steamed
  Dumplings, 112
Vincent's Spaghetti, 121
Potatoes
  Cat Noir's Mashed Potatoes
    and Sausage, 123
  Colombo de Poulet, 119
  Marinette Soup, 97
  Potato-Leek Soup, 98
  Salade Parisienne, 99
  Tartiflette, 90
Pound It! Cake, 41
Puff pastry
  King's Cake, 35
  Sweetheart Vol-au-Vents
    with Wild Mushroom–
    Chicken Filling, 125–26
  Tiny Tuna Tarts, 74

Q

**Quiche, Sabine's Salmon
  and Spinach,** 116

R

Radishes
  French Bistro Salad, 100
  Radishes with Herbed
    Butter and Salt, 70

S

Salads
  French Bistro Salad, 100
  Salade Parisienne, 99
**Salmon and Spinach
  Quiche, Sabine's,** 116
Sandwiches
  Camembert Croque Monsieur, 84

Grilled Cheese and
  Tomato Soup, 89
Sausage
  Cat Noir's Mashed Potatoes
    and Sausage, 123
  Kung Food's Pepperoni
    Pizza Sword, 107–9
Seafood
  Sabine's Salmon and
    Spinach Quiche, 116
  Shrimp Scampi Skewers, 73
  Tiny Tuna Tarts, 74
  Uncle Wang's Steamed
    Dumplings, 112
Seaweed Soup, Special-Powers, 94
Sherbet, Orange, 136
Shrimp
  Shrimp Scampi Skewers, 73
  Uncle Wang's Steamed
    Dumplings, 112
Soufflé, Simple Cheese, 129
Soupe à l'Oignon Gratinée, 87
Soups
  French Onion Soup, 87
  Grilled Cheese and
    Tomato Soup, 89
  Marinette Soup, 97
  Potato-Leek Soup, 98
  Special-Powers Seaweed Soup, 94
Spaghetti, Vincent's, 121
Spinach
  Sabine's Salmon and
    Spinach Quiche, 116
  Salade Parisienne, 99
Strawberries
  Birthday Cake for Adrien, 50–52
  Derby Hat Cake, 45–47
  Marinette's Birthday Cake, 49
  Strawberry Ice Cream, 136
  Strawberry with Chocolate
    Chip Ice Cream, 136

Sweet potatoes
  Colombo de Poulet, 119
  Marinette Soup, 97

T

Tartiflette, 90
Tarts
  Tiny Tuna Tarts, 74
  Tom's Tarte aux Fruits, 28
Tofu
  Special-Powers Seaweed Soup, 94
Tomatoes
  Cheese-and-Vegetable
    Pesto Pizza, 110–11
  Grilled Cheese and
    Tomato Soup, 89
  Ladybug Canapés, 69
  Vincent's Spaghetti, 121
Tuna Tarts, Tiny, 74

V

Vanilla Bean Ice Cream, 136
Vegetables. *See also specific vegetables*
  Cheese-and-Vegetable
    Pesto Pizza, 110–11
Vichyssoise, 98
Vinaigrette, Mustard-Shallot, 100

W

Wheat Stalk Bread, 14–16

PO Box 3088
San Rafael, CA 94912
www.insighteditions.com

Find us on Facebook: www.facebook.com/InsightEditions

Follow us on Instagram: @insighteditions

Miraculous™ is a trademark of MIRACULOUS CORP
© 2025 MIRACULOUS CORP. ALL RIGHTS RESERVED.

All rights reserved. Published by Insight Editions, San Rafael, California, in 2025. No part of this book may be reproduced in any form without written permission from the publisher.

ISBN: 979-8-88663-910-0

Publisher: Raoul Goff
SVP, Group Publisher: Vanessa Lopez
VP, Creative: Chrissy Kwasnik
VP, Manufacturing: Alix Nicholaeff
Publishing Director: Mike Degler
Editorial Director: Thom O'Hearn
Managing Editor: Shannon Ballesteros
Art Director: Stuart Smith
Assistant Editor: Sami Alvarado
Production Manager: Deena Hashem
Strategic Production Planner: Lina s Palma-Temena

Recipes by Lisa Kingsley, Waterbury Publications, Inc.
Written by S. T. Bende
Photography by Ken Carlson, Waterbury Publications, Inc.

Insight Editions, in association with Roots of Peace, will plant two trees for each tree used in the manufacturing of this book. Roots of Peace is an internationally renowned humanitarian organization dedicated to eradicating land mines worldwide and converting war-torn lands into productive farms and wildlife habitats. Roots of Peace will plant two million fruit and nut trees in Afghanistan and provide farmers there with the skills and support necessary for sustainable land use.

Manufactured in China by Insight Editions
10 9 8 7 6 5 4 3 2 1